# TAKE OWNERSHIP

MONEY MATTERS MONDAYS | BUILDING KINGDOM WEALTH

VOLUME 2

HENRIETTA ENGLAND

Edited by
NICOLE QUEEN

VISION PUBLISHING
HOUSE

Vision Publishing House
www.vision-publishinghouse.com

ISBN: 978-1-955297-51-6 (Paperback)

We don't talk about trees getting older. We say they are growing. Let's use the same term for ourselves: We're not getting older, we're just growing! That's the spirit of living. We serve a living God.

— HENRIETTA ENGLAND

# CONTENTS

# A WORD FROM THE AUTHOR

In this book, we will define ownership, begin exploring purchasing or refinancing your home, and differentiate entities of credit approval process. What does a lender/underwriter look for to qualify you for income, reserves, and assets? These are key resource tools in building a complete financial portfolio.

We will further explore planning for retirement, savings, and investments, as well as mistakes to avoid while planning for your future. Most importantly, we will dive into how to maintain an excellent credit and FICO score. Now you may be saying, "I don't have an excellent credit score" or "What is a FICO score?" Well, this book will give you detailed information on how to begin to repair your credit and boost your credit and FICO score.

In today's society, the scammers and hackers are busy trying to clone, steal, and confiscate your identity. So you must equip yourself and your household with the knowledge, understanding, and wisdom on how to protect your household from fraud and identity theft.

The goal after reading this book is to learn to apply these principles to your everyday life, for you to be able to decide if you are ready for a new home purchase, or should you continue renting and saving for the biggest investment for you and your family. Purchasing a home is one of the biggest investments we make in a lifetime, and it can be very intimidating when you have never experienced the requirements and documentation needed for a final loan approval. This process is repeated when you decide to refinance your existing home or decide on pulling down some of the equity in your current home. It is important to protect oneself in every arena in your life, to be prepared and ready for whatever may come your way, and to build a sustainable financial portfolio, which will exhibit your personal and business integrity, as you move forward in becoming economically stable, fiscally fit, and provide a transformation that will last a lifetime for you and your household.

Let's begin.

# WHO WE ARE: TRI-FOLD CONNECTIONS

*Tri-Fold Connection's mission* is to prepare everyone (regardless of race, creed, color, age, culture, religion, or denomination) for an abundant life. We do this by changing the mindset to be prepared, to acquire new skills in financial stability, and to create kingdom wealth, God's way.

We empower our clients with Biblical principles, precepts, and encouragement to achieve their goals, dreams, visions, and assignments. We coach you to effectively use your time, talent, and treasures to work for you to live life the way God intended in abundance, overflow, and prosperity.

We aspire to educate adolescents, young adults, adults, seniors, and people with disabilities on economic growth and development and creditworthiness, with our primary focus on financial literacy. Our motto is fiscal fitness, and our goal is for you to have a transformation lasting a lifetime™.

We desire to become your accountability coach, partner with you, and help you to design success for you and your legacy. We offer a variety of services, and your initial consultation is free.

Contact us via:

Website: www.trifoldconnectionsllc.com
Email: info@trifoldconnectionsllc.com
Phone: 708-553-0002

Scan below to access your complimentary gift (Features of Your Dream Home + Home Inspection Worksheets) or visit my website.

COMPLIMENTARY WORKSHEETS

TRI FOLD CONNECTIONS WEBSITE

# 1

# TAKE OWNERSHIP

> The heavens are thine, the earth also is thine: as for the world and the fullness thereof, thou hast founded them.
>
> — PSALM 89:11 KJV

*Ownership* is defined as the act, state, or right of possessing something. The meaning of ownership is the state, relation, or fact of being an owner or a group or organization of owners. The characteristics of ownership means to constitute possession; the owner must be entitled to the possession of the property, and have the right to maintain the thing that he/she owns. There are ownership types such as the legal right of an individual, group, corporation, or government to possess a certain matter. The subject of ownership has two main components: material and immaterial things. Material ownership is that which is tangible. Tangible is perceptible by touch, physical property, land, car, books, keys, phone, etc. Immaterial ownership is spiritual rather than physical (put a pin in this thought; we will elaborate further in coming volumes).

Ownership is acquired by *occupation and by intellectual creation.* Ownership and other real rights over property are acquired and transmitted by law, donation, estate, and intestate succession (a will or not having a will), and in consequence of certain contracts, by tradition. To take ownership is a big responsibility. Ownership is the ability to own a situation, outcome, or an event. Responsibility is to take accountability for one's actions, an opportunity or ability to act independently and make decisions without authorization, or a moral obligation to behave correctly toward or in respect of a person.

Meanwhile, taking ownership is viable because it builds trust, support, and relationships with people you care about. A team or household cannot thrive without a lifestyle of accountability because it's what keeps the team working together toward a collective goal, which defines the organizational mission. Ownership and accountability need individuals working together for the quality and success of both the output and outcomes of their work together. Both of these are equally important as ownership does not stand for perfection.

There is a difference when absolute ownership comes into play. Absolute ownership is used to describe ownership of land interests, meaning that interest(s) or share(s) are owned by the person. Absolute interests are not subject to any other restrictions or orders (not in a trust, not a remainder interest, or a life interest). Lastly, ownership involves the absolute rights and legitimate claim to a tangible object. It means to own a tangible object by the owner. Possession is more of the physical control of the tangible object. The possessor has a better claim to the title of the object than anyone, except the owner him/herself (Oxford Dictionary).

To purchase a home is a big deal. There are substantial benefits for first-time home buyers. The initial preparation and documentation can be an overwhelming process. To prepare for one of the biggest purchases that you will make in your lifetime, there is a process. One must have all financial matters in order as well as knowledge of credit score and FICO score six months prior to the purchase. This is where the "art of budgeting" comes into play (see volume 1). To properly manage well, a budget is essential. In my career, I have seen where the lender/underwriter may very well ask the borrower for up to six months of bank statements. This is to ensure you are budgeting and managing well your existing household income. Household income is the combined net income of all people sharing a particular household or place of residence. It includes every form of income (e.g., salaries and wages earned, retirement income, near-cash government transfers like Social Security, EBT [electronic benefit transfer—food stamps], and investment gains [dividend income, etc.]). In a household, it is not necessary for individuals in question to be related in any way to be considered members of the same household.

### Income Qualifications

A budget will reflect on your bank statements. Why is budgeting so important? A budget is important to help you manage your finances well. A budget allows you to dictate to your money how you want it to perform for you and not the other way around. A budget holds you accountable and responsible for your household income. It allows you to allocate funds into different savings and investment instruments.

When you begin to prepare to purchase your new home, you must start by having reserves and other assets. Assets are equivalent to cash on hand. This vehicle allows for fast liquidity, if necessary. The underwriter will require a budget letter for saved funds. This letter should include documentation from the bank or credit union where your funds are being held. The underwriter requires three months (not excluding up to six months) of documentation, meaning the funds have been on deposit in your financial institution for ninety days or more. They also call these types of funds seasoned funds. This is why it is so important to begin saving now. If the funds are not seasoned, the underwriter will request documentation of those funds (i.e. canceled check, copy of front and back of check, bank statement).

Having in place a six-month reserve for emergencies looks good to the underwriter and speaks to your integrity when it comes down to accountability and responsibility to repay the mortgage note. As I just mentioned, the underwriter only requires ninety days or three months of reserves. *It's better to have it and not need it than to need it and not have it.* The aforementioned statement is what my Aunt Imogene used to say to me often as a teenager growing up. I found this statement to be true many times over.

You will also be required to have two months of bank statements dated within forty-five days of the mortgage application. The 1003 Form is Fannie Mae's form number for the Uniform Residential Loan Application (URLA). Freddie Mac refers to this as Form 65. The URLA, 1003, and Form 65 are all the same forms and serve as a mortgage loan application. This includes checking, savings, and money market accounts. This is to verify that you have sufficient funds available for the down payment, closing costs associated with the loan, and reserve/assets requirements (as I previously mentioned in the above paragraph). If you are to receive gift funds, you will be required to have a donor letter. This letter must include the donor's name, address, phone number, and their relationship to you, the borrower. The donor must also state that the funds are a gift and not a debt to be paid back. If the donor states that it is a debt to be repaid at a later date, then this debt must be included in your debt-to-income ratios, which could cause you to not qualify for the loan.

Debt-to-income ratios will make or break any deal on the table. Debt-to-income ratios are simply how much debt you owe versus how much household income is earned. Typically, the debt-to-income ratio is 30/42, with 30% of income available versus 42% of indebtedness. Depending on the amount of the gift, the donor may also have to provide a bank statement to show the underwriter that the funds are seasoned. If the funds are not seasoned from your donor, the donor will have to show documentation of receipt of those funds. Getting a six-month head start in planning for one of the biggest purchases in one's life is important in more ways than you may understand.

With retirement/brokerage assets, you will need up to two months of these statements also dated within forty-five days of the actual mortgage application. Retirement/brokerage assets are used for reserve and/or assets only.

I've provided some key points to consider, which will help enhance your understanding of this procedure, or any lending process involving different financial institutions or credit unions.

*Lending Process Tips to Consider:*

- Be aware that retirement and/or brokerage funds are calculated differently. Meaning, that the underwriter does not count them at face value.

- Reserves are terms of liquidation for 401(k), pension, and insurance funds being used for reserves.

- Retirement accounts are calculated at 60% of face value, brokerage assets at 70% of the value, and record other non-cash/non-retirement funds at 70% of their face value (e.g., stocks, bonds, trades, insurance policy, etc.). These funds must be liquidated prior to closing (if you are using these funds to qualify for the loan).

- If you are selling a home when purchasing your new home, you will be required to provide the *net proceeds* from the sale of your existing home. You must also provide in the notes the anticipated date of the sale of that home. All this information can be acquired through your mortgage loan officer or real estate broker.

- Personal Property Sold: If you are selling off personal property to meet closing cost requirements, you are required to show proof of the bill of sale and/or receipt of funds (Note: Be prepared to show documentation of funds via direct deposit, check, Zelle, PayPal, Venmo or CashApp. Make a copy of the check and/or be prepared to show recorded transaction). More is better. It's better to have it and not need it than to need it and not have it. Otherwise, you will not be able to use the funds as qualifying assets.

- Closing Disclosure: Verifying the sale of your home. This can be done at the closing table. The mortgage loan officer will need to make a note to the underwriter when this home will close and the expected net proceeds, including the date of availability.

- Large Deposits: If you deposit a significant amount into your account, you will need to provide evidence or verification to the underwriter regarding the source of these funds. *If you have no documentation, the large deposit cannot be used as qualifying assets.*

- Secured Loan Proceeds: You are required to provide the following documentation: a copy of the note, proceeds of the check, evidence of the deposit, proof of ownership of the collateral, and evidence of the value of the collateral.

- Trust funds are an acceptable means of qualifying for the reserve income requirement. If you are the holder of the trust agreement, you will need a complete trust agreement or letter from the trustee verifying full access by the applicant.

- You will also be required to show documentation and verify proof of an earnest money check. A canceled earnest money check for the down payment should be accompanied by the respective bank statement to provide proof of the fund's source.

Now, let's look at normal income qualifications for a loan. You will be required to provide thirty days of salary and/or hourly pay stubs dated within thirty days of the loan application. Provide the underwriter or loan processor with two years of W-2s of the most current year, complete with a physical tax return, signed and dated. If you are self-employed, commission 25%+, employed by the family, or OTR (over-the-road) truck driver, you will be required to provide two years' complete personal and business tax returns, signed and dated. If you have filed for an extension, you must provide IRS (Internal Revenue Service) form 4868 or E-extension filing for the most recent tax year filing not completed by April 15 of the current year. As the borrower, if you have experienced gaps in employment, the underwriter will request a letter of explanation (LOX) for any gaps in employment.

I have shared with you the income qualification to make a large purchase, purchase your own home, refinance your existing home, or any loan requested from a financial institution, credit union, or loan store. This information is helpful for you and your household.

**What Is a Portfolio?**

A portfolio is a range of investments held by a person or organization. It is a compilation of materials that exemplifies your beliefs, skills, qualifications, education, training, and experience. It provides insight into your personality and work ethic. It is also a grouping of financial assets such as stocks, bonds, commodities, currencies, and cash equivalents as well as their fund counterparts, including mutual, exchange-traded, and closed funds. Portfolios are held by investors and/or managed by financial professionals and money .

Tri Fold Connections has been celebrated by the Albert Nelson Marquis Who's Who in America for Excellence in Financial Advising and Education in 2023.

Scan the QR below to read the article celebrating our success.

### How Do You Build a Portfolio?

There are ten steps to build a complete financial portfolio:

1. Craft a balance sheet.
2. Contribute to your 401(k).
3. Pay off credit card debt and installment debt.
4. Open a Roth IRA.
5. Purchase a home.
6. Build six months' worth of emergency funds.
7. Look into other investments.
8. Invest in yourself.
9. Save for your children's education (empty nesters, save for your bucket list adventures).
10. Stay the course.

### How to Best Use Your Resources to Serve God, Family, & Others

As we bring this chapter to a close, there are biblical principles and precepts I will share with you. A principle is a fundamental truth or proposition that serves as the foundation for a system of belief or behavior for a chain of reasoning, or in layman's terms, the law, a rule, or a code of conduct. A precept is a general rule intended to regulate behavior or thought. In the biblical content, *precept* is a commandment, instruction, or order intended as an authoritative rule of action.

In taking ownership, there are rules, guidelines, policies, and procedures to follow. It is the same if you desire to become prosperous, healthy, wealthy, and wise. The instructions are clear, but many choose not to follow the instructions.

When a spiritual or natural law is broken, there is cause and effect. If you go speeding down the highway, you know the police will pull you over and issue you a speeding violation warning and/or ticket. That ticket will cost you time and money. If you take a plant from its source (the dirt), it will soon wither and die.

There are twenty-one spiritual laws in God's Kingdom. I will discuss five of these laws for a more in-depth understanding.

1. Law of Mutual Forgiveness:

> For if ye forgive men their trespasses, your heavenly Father will also forgive you, but if ye forgive not men their trespasses, neither will your Father forgive your trespasses.
>
> — MATTHEW 6:14–15 (KJV)

Our God forgives those who forgive others. Forgiving others is not always the easiest thing to do. Forgiveness is spiritual and not natural. Man's natural response is to get even or plot a plan of revenge for the offense. I offer you another perspective. If you refuse to forgive an offense, that is the same measure you will be judged before our Heavenly Father. Forgiveness is not for the other person. Forgiveness is for you, for you to be able to move forward freely and without regret or remorse.

2. Law of Having What We Say (Law of Faith)

> And Jesus answering saith unto them, 'Have faith in God. For verily I say unto you, That whosoever shall say unto this mountain, Be thou removed, and be thou cast into the sea; and shall not doubt in his heart, but shall believe that those things which he saith shall come to pass; he shall have whatsoever he saith. Therefore I say unto you, What things soever ye desire when ye pray, believe that ye receive them, and ye shall have them.'
>
> — MARK 11:22–24 (KJV)

We will always get what we say when we believe without doubt or wavering in our hearts. This is a spiritual law. What we say carries weight. We have the power of life in death in our tongues. We can sow positive speech or negative speech, and either way, the seed will come forth. Faith is also spiritual. One must exercise faith. Faith is action and movement, calling the things you don't see into your tangible existence, meaning calling the unseen to show up to be seen.

Here's one of many testimonies I will share with you. My father drove a Cadillac ever since I can remember, as a girl growing up. I remember saying I wanted to drive a Cadillac, just like my dad. Well, my dad passed on in 1989, and as I matured in my faith and released forgiveness, in 2017, I purchased my brand-new Cadillac for half the sticker price. That was the Law of Faith in the full revelation of the unseen being called to the seen. We must put our faith to work.

3. Law of Giving and Receiving.

> Honor the LORD with thy substance, And with the first fruits of all thine increase: So shall thy barns be

> filled with plenty, And thy presses shall burst out with new wine.
>
> — PROVERBS 3:9–10 (KJV)

You cannot beat God's giving, no matter how hard you try. The more you give to God, the more He'll give to you. When we give God our first and our best in our time, talent, and treasure, God will bless us abundantly, exceedingly—more than we could ever ask, think, or imagine in our wildest dreams (Ephesians 3:20). Wow, just think about that for a minute! What have you been asking God for in secret? Are you giving God your first and your best? It's important that we give God what he requires by law (Malachi 3:10).

It's equally important that we realize when we are given more, more is required (Luke 12:48). It is expected of us to use our time, talents, treasure, wealth, knowledge, and the like to glorify God and to benefit others. This is a perfect opportunity to show God that we are faithful stewards of God's grace in its various forms (1 Peter 4:10).

No one should assume that the less we know about God and His gifts, the less God will require of us. No, we are to learn and seek knowledge to understand Jesus's parables. We are held accountable and responsible for knowing our master's will for our lives. God has plainly shown us what He requires — "No, O people, the LORD has told you what is good, and this is what he requires of you: to do what is right, to love mercy, and to walk humbly with your God" (Micah 6:8 (NLT).

4. Law of Sowing and Reaping

> Be not deceived; God is not mocked: for whatsoever a man soweth, that shall he also reap. For he that soweth

> to his flesh shall of the flesh reap corruption; but he that soweth to the Spirit reap life everlasting.
>
> — GALATIANS 6:7–8 (KJV)

Do not be fooled, whatever you desire of ill will upon or toward someone else, you will also experience many times worse than what you desired for another. I remember my mom saying to me as a little girl, "If a person is digging a ditch for me, they may as well dig two." I asked her why. "Because the same ditch they are plotting or planning for me, they too shall be in the same ditch." So, if we sow to the flesh, we will reap fleshly returns.

Now, if we sow to the Spirit (meaning Holy Spirit), we shall reap a harvest of much fruit, some twenty, sixty, and a hundredfold blessings (Matthew 13:8–9, NLT). Still, other seeds fell on fertile soil, and they produced a crop that was thirty, sixty, and even a hundred times as much as had been planted! Anyone with ears to hear should listen and understand. Other references include Luke 8:8, Mark 4:20, Matthew 13:23, and Matthew 19:29.

When applying these principles (wisdom), you can expect a return on what you have sown. When the Bible mentions receiving a harvest of thirty times more or thirtyfold, it's referring to the square root in multiplication (a number that produces a specified quantity when multiplied by itself).

5. Law of Restoration

> Men do not despise a thief, if he steal to satisfy his soul when he is hungry; But if he be found, he shall restore seven-fold; He shall give all thy substance of his house.
>
> — PROVERBS 6:30–31 (KJV)

> If someone steals from you and your household, they must pay back seven times the amount that was stolen or to the square root of seven, which is forty-nine times. This is God's recompense, God's justice, God's restitution for those who honor God and submit to the will of God. There's no need to take revenge for the Law will avenge itself.
>
> Just a note I would like to share: "Never give from your cup [meaning if you need the funds for a bill, keep it, because if that person doesn't pay you back, then you are short on your needs, and this typically will cause strife and/or division]. Always lend from your overflow [funds that you have in surplus or profit]."
>
> *** To find all twenty-one spiritual laws of God's Kingdom, go to: www.eternallibrary.org.*

When you begin to read your Bible in-depth, you will see that Jesus said more about money than any other topic of heaven and hell combined. Our attitude toward money and our personal resources says so much about our lives and how we live. Money is a tool to provide for your needs and to help with the needs of others. God blesses us to become the blessing in someone else's life. Giving should flow from the heart of man, a heart that desires to help the widows, poor, needy, and fatherless children. Money should not be used to draw attention to ourselves, but instead, it should be used as the tool and resource it is. Proper management and budgeting will allow you an opportunity to save, invest, give, and then watch God, and how He will increase your resources to give even more.

We should strive to think beyond our earthly life and share what we have been given in order to help advance the Kingdom of God right here on earth, establish the Kingdom economy, and rebuild the commonwealth of the Kingdom.

Psalm 24:1 (GNB) says, "The world and all that is in it belong to the LORD; the earth and all who live on it are His." The question is, do you trust God? Trusting God as your source takes a leap of faith. According to Nelson's Bible Dictionary, *faith* is a belief in or confident attitude toward God, involving commitment to His will for one's life. Nelson also says *belief* is to place one's trust in God's truth.

I remember when I was being set out, I didn't know what to do. I prayed and asked God for direction and listened to the instructions. Next thing I knew, me and my household were trailing the moving truck to our new location. This house was likened to a mini-mansion. It was only my two daughters, my aunt Ruth, my dog Precious, and me in this home with seven bedrooms (two master bedrooms) quad level, four bathrooms, living room, formal dining room, kitchen, family room, and lower-level entertainment space. Now you know nobody could have pulled this off but God. We stayed there until I purchased our very own single-family home in 2001, which was also another miracle. A special thank-you to Lewis Darling, the angel God sent to provide shelter for my family and me.

I've been in banking since I was eighteen years old. I became a mortgage loan officer when I was in my early thirties. I had never sent one of my clients to the closing table without instructions to purchase a cashier's check for the closing cost. I went to the closing table without a cashier's check and walked away from the closing table with a cashier's check payable to me for close to $3,000 dollars, to God be the glory! I remember it like it was yesterday. I went out and purchased new family room furniture and took my family and Precious, our family dog, on a mini vacation. I have said all this to encourage you to trust God. Trust the process! Both the natural and spiritual laws work when observed and obeyed. God owns it all, and He will supply more than enough for you and your household.

Here are some passages of scripture to encourage you to stay the course and receive your full inheritance.

> Now to him who is able to do immeasurably more than all we ask or image, according to his power that is at work within us.
>
> — EPHESIANS 3:20 NIV

> And we know that in all things God works for the good of those who love him, who have been called according to his purpose. For those God foreknew he also predestined to be conformed to the image of his Son, that he might be the firstborn among many brothers and sisters. And those he predestined, he also called; those he called, he also justified; those he justified, he also glorified.
>
> — ROMANS 8:28–30 NIV

It's easy for us to give when we know we will receive something in return. Jesus challenges you and me to remember that giving from the heart should not have any strings attached. When you give a gift to someone in need, you should not go around bragging to everyone what you have done (Matthew 6:2–4 MSG). What you do in secret, God will reward you openly. God is working behind the scenes and preparing blessing upon blessing that you will not have room to contain.

Paul earned his living as a tentmaker during his missionary journey. Paul was grateful for the financial support he received from some of the church members and others in the villages. Paul was careful to not become a financial burden to the believers in the church of Philippi, where he was preaching and teaching the gospel free of charge. Regardless of his circumstances, we can all learn from Paul today. Having enough does not bring contentment; being content makes what you have enough.

*Contentment is contingent on our attitudes and how we perceive our situations.* As you lay your resources before the Lord, ask, "Lord, am I using my resources in a way you would have given me to accomplish your purpose? If your answer is yes, you should thank God for his wisdom and provision for you and your household, and you should aspire to continue to grow in giving. If your answer is no, then self-condemnation and regret are not the proper response. The Good News is that God, who is faithful and just, forgives you. He is ready to help you direct your time, talent, and treasure to provide a transformation of how to use your money and help you become a better money manager.

So where do you start? You go back to the heart of the matter. There's a decision you have to make. Whom will you serve? Are you serving God with your resources? Or, are you serving yourself? Jesus tells us that no man can serve two masters. Either he will hate the one and love the other, or he will be devoted to the one and despise the other. We cannot serve both God and money (Matthew 6:24).

* * *

***Prayer of Thanksgiving for Financial Resources***

*Gracious Father, I come before You on this day to say thank You. I adore you, God. You are the Great I AM. You are the Wonderful Counselor, King of kings, Lord of lords, mighty in battle, Jehovah Shalom, and my peace. You are Jehovah Jireh, my provider.*

*Father God, if I have done anything to sin against you, my sister, or my brother, by omission or commission, I ask for forgiveness, God. I desire to have a clean heart and renew a right spirit within me. Thank you, God, for keeping me and my household all week long. Thank you for protecting my/our residence. Thank you, God, for safety, as I/we travel to work, appointments, and my/our leisure activities. Thank you, God, that you keep all children safe as they travel to and from school, play, entertainment, and social and spiritual events (God-ordained).*

*Thank You, God, that I (and my household) have food to eat, clothes to wear, and shoes on my (our) feet. Thank you, God, that we have a bed to sleep in. Thank You, God, that You take care of me (us) day in and day out. Thank You, God, that You never grow weary. I thank You, God, for good health and strength. I thank You, God, for the activity of my limbs, so that I can move, breathe, and have my very being. I thank You, God, for the ability to make sound strategic decisions and stick to the plans. I thank You for supernatural debt cancellation. I thank You that I shall exercise self-discipline and self-control in all areas of my life daily, specifically in the area of my finances.*

*Help me to become a good steward of my financial resources. Help me to grow in faith, believing, trusting, and obeying Your principles and precepts. Let my faith be BIGGER than my fears. I thank You for an accountability partner, a person who will be diligent and help me and my household to reach our goals. Help us to seek wise counsel, godly counsel. We place our plans before You, God, for You are the chief executive officer, and we know You have our best interest at heart.*

*Now, God, I ask that You blow a fresh wind on my (our) goals, dreams, assignments, and vision. Without You, I/we would fail. With You, all things are possible. What seems impossible to me/us is possible with You as the head of my/our life. We thank You in advance that I/we can speak a word that can change the trajectory of my/our life, according to my/our faith.*

*I ask for an overflow of blessings to every person(s)/ household reading this book. I thank You in advance that as they set goals and dreams before You in this decade, they will look back at their journey and see the manifestations of Your promises fulfilled in their lives.*

*Now, God, help us to get debt-free, free from any bondages holding us back from the blessings that You have in store for all of us. I bind up the enemies' attack to try and come and steal this word of knowledge. I bind any retaliatory demon and cast them back into the abyss of utter darkness from whence they came. I seal these prayers and the unspoken prayers of my heart in Jesus's blood and His righteousness.*

*In the authority of Jesus, we pray. Amen.*

FUTURE

## 2

# SAVINGS AND INVESTMENT OVERVIEW

> Save when there shall be no poor among you; for the Lord shall greatly bless thee in the land which the Lord thy God giveth thee for an inheritance to possess it.
>
> — DEUTERONOMY 15:4 KJV

It is important that we start off the right way, but it is imperative that we end the right way. We left off in Chapter 1 talking about your financial resources and had an outline for building a complete financial portfolio. Savings and investments are keys to economic growth and development, financial stability, and prepared readiness. We will further explore key elements that affect our ability to save, invest, borrow, and trade.

### Federal Prime Lending Rate

As of May 4, 2023, the Bank of America NA prime rate is 8.25%, according to the bank's website. We have seen a steady increase in the prime lending rate since 2022. The Federal Reserve has zero patience and will continue to hike its benchmark interest rate to ease investors' minds and to avoid the market crashing altogether. The present inflation rate as of September 2023 is 3.7%, and the normal inflation rate is at 2% when the economy is experiencing growth and stability. This is one of the reasons the Federal Reserve is continuing to raise the prime lending rate to level out our economy. The average APR (annual percentage rate) for all credit cards as of May 2023 is 28.24% heading into the second quarter, according to LendingTree.com. In December 2022, the average rate on all new credit card offers was 20.82%, up from 20.17%, according to the Federal Reserve. This is not good news for consumers who are carrying debt month to month because you will see an increase in the minimum payment due, which results in higher monthly expenses and directly affects your household's ability to save and invest for future endeavors.

> *Note*: The annual percentage rates (APR) you pay on your own credit cards might differ from the national average. Credit card APRs can vary widely based on several factors, such as credit score, FICO score, and debt-to-income ratio, just to name some of the key factors where APR is affected.

On the flip side of the Federal Reserve increasing the prime lending rate, its goal is to bring stability to the economy. We are growing and maturing in economic awareness. Economics is all about you and me; it tells a detailed story of how we as a people:

- Manage our resources
- Manage our spending habits
- Manage our money
- Manage our waste
- Track our app use on the different apps we have in use, for our convenience

Becoming an economist requires building new skills and a new mindset, which are foundational to our growth, stability, productivity, and prosperity. Let us plow forward, fully committed to reinvigorating the economy of our day, to give new energy or strength, and to create and bring forth the following:

- Economic stability
- Economic growth
- Economic development
- Workforce development and human capital
- Individual asset-building approaches
- Approaches for improving housing affordability
- Service integration and multigenerational approaches
- Approaches to improve food insecurity in school settings

An economist is an expert in economics. Economics is a branch of knowledge concerned with the production, consumption, and transfer of wealth and the condition of a region or group with regard to material prosperity.

As consumers, we must be prepared and ready for anything that is thrown our way to protect ourselves and the stability of the household. Although the federal funds rate (also known as the prime lending rate) is the rate at which banks charge one another for short-term borrowing, it is not the rate that consumers pay. The Federal Reserve's movements still have a direct effect on borrowing and saving rates. The upside of the decision to raise the benchmark is your interest received on savings, money markets, certificates of deposit, individual retirement accounts, and the like is on the rise. With the rise in the benchmark rate, you can expect higher APRs when making purchases. This directly affects the consumers' ability to save and invest more in future endeavors. This is surely a good time for each individual to reassess your budget and spending power.

According to bankrate.com, as of May 9, 2023, the top five savings accounts are offered online at PNC Bank, Synchrony Bank, Capital One, Citizens Bank, and CITI Bank. When you are searching for an avenue to save and invest, it's a good rule of thumb to search online rates versus the rates being offered inside your financial institutions. As a consumer, you should aim to secure a deposit rate that at least beats the going rate of inflation.

Here are some key factors you want to consider when assessing your needs for your household. The general rule of thumb is to keep your spending on necessities, such as food and housing, to no more than 50% of your take-home pay. This is based on the 50/30/20 rule. This rule recommends spending 50% of your income on basic necessities, 30% on discretionary items (nonessential items: recreation, entertainment, or other items consumers purchase when they have money left over after necessary expenses are covered), and stashing the other 20% away as savings or investment in your future endeavors. The end result is to have a six-month emergency cash reserve on hand.

### Automobile Loans

Due to the Federal Reserve raising the benchmark rate, as I stated earlier, it affects automobile purchases as well as student loans. Let us openly discuss automobile loans. When you have decided to purchase that new or used vehicle, your credit score and FICO score need to be in good to excellent standing (670–850 credit score). The APR you receive will reflect your present credit score. The daily interest rate is based on credit score, income, and the term of the loan (debt-to-income ratio). If you desire to have a long-term loan, expect a higher interest rate. If you already have an excellent credit score, you will have an opportunity for the best rates available. The lender will often factor in additional fees, so be sure to carefully read over the loan term agreement and promissory note. Automobile loans are generally fixed-rate loans, payable over equally monthly installments. For current interest rates and APR, go to bankrate.com.

When shopping for that new or used vehicle, remember to know your credit score and FICO score prior to the purchase. Why is this important? This is important because you do not want every lender pulling your credit report. This has a negative impact on your credit score and will cause your scores to decrease for too many recent inquiries.

Work smarter, not harder. Do your homework. Be prepared and be ready. In preparation for the big purchase, shop around; don't take the first offer, even if it is what you have budgeted for the purchase. Avoid being haggled or rushed when you are signing paperwork, and be sure to read everything you sign. Yes, everything you sign. The bottom line is simply a car loan is an agreement between the lender and you, the borrower, which allows you to borrow money for the sole purpose of purchasing that vehicle over an agreed-upon term or length of time.

### Student Loans

Student loans have always been an avenue for students to pay for higher education. Now, many students globally are trying to find ways to get on top of this surmounting debt. Rapidly, the rising cost of college tuition and inflation have made student debt the only option to pay for higher learning. When shopping for a student loan, know there are four types of federal student loans to consider:

- Direct subsidized loans
- Direct unsubsidized loans
- Direct PLUS loans
- Direct consolidation loans

A direct, subsidized loan is available to eligible undergraduate students with demonstrated financial need. Your financial need is determined with a formula provided on the FAFSA (Free Application for Federal Student Aid). If approved, no credit check is needed.

Direct unsubsidized loans are similar to subsidized loans with some key differences. You, the borrower, are responsible for paying the interest that accuses during all periods, even when the loan is not in active repayment. Another benefit of this loan type is that it is available to both undergraduate and graduate students, and eligibility is not based on financial need.

A direct PLUS Loan is made to either the graduate or professional students, also known as grad PLUS loan, or parents of dependent undergraduate students, also called the parent PLUS Loan. The purpose of this loan is to fill the gap between the cost of attendance and available resources if you still require additional funding (cash) to pay for your education after borrowing your maximum limit of unsubsidized and subsidized loans. A credit check is required. If you have an adverse credit history reflection on your report, you may be able to still get approval for PLUS Loan funding either with a cosigner, also called an endorser, or by meeting other guideline criteria.

Lastly, direct consolidation loans are slightly different than the other types of federal loans. This loan type allows borrowers to combine all eligible federal student loans into a single loan, which typically takes place after the student has graduated, and there is no application fee. Consolidation loans are income-driven repayment plans, and some other options are available, such as loan forgiveness programs.

President Biden has approved the student loan forgiveness package. Now, he has the executive ability to cancel all debt. Student loans were the one source of debt that did not add extra weight to Americans' debt load in the second quarter, researchers noted. The Biden administration has moved forward with the plan to cancel $10K per borrower and up to $20K per borrower, depending on income qualifications. This would bring relief to millions of borrowers. Here's what you can expect from student loan forgiveness:

- $10,000 of student loan cancellation for federal student loans

- PELL Grant recipients $20,000 in student loan forgiveness

- All federal student loans would qualify for student loan relief, including direct loans, FFELP Loans, Perkins Loans, Parent PLUS Loans, and grad PLUS Loans

- Income threshold of $150,000 for individual student loan borrowers and $250,000 for families

- Student loan cancellation is as early as forty-five days for student loan borrowers whose income is on file with the US Department of Education (lendingtree.com)

- As of May 8, 2023, the U.S. Department of Education Secretary announced that it has approved a total of $42 billion in Public Service Loan Forgiveness (PSLF) for more than 615,000 borrowers since October 2021. This is a direct result of the temporary PSLF changes made by the Biden-Harris Administration that made it easier for borrowers to reach forgiveness. (*Note*: The Supreme Court ruling will directly affect the forgiveness program.)

- Essential dates to remember are August 31 and December 31. Visit www.edu.gov to stay informed.

While most students rely on federally funded loans with a fixed rate, more than 1.4 million students a year use private student loans to bridge the gap between the cost of college and their financial aid and savings.

As we bring this chapter to a close, I will share encouraging scriptures and a word of prayer to keep you and your household empowered and enlightened to continue moving forward in building "Kingdom Wealth," God's way, with the knowledge of taking ownership in this season of your life and lifestyle, to provide you and your household a "transformation lasting a lifetime." TM

## A Living Sacrifice to God

> And so, dear brothers and sisters, I plead with you to give your bodies to God because of all he has done for you. Let them be a living and holy sacrifice-the kind he will find acceptable. This is truly the way to worship him. Don't copy the behavior and customs of this world, but let God transform you into a new person by changing the way you think. Then you will learn to know God's will for you, which is good and pleasing and perfect.
>
> — ROMANS 12:1–2 NLT

Wherever your treasure is, there the desires of your heart will also be. Your eye is like a lamp that provides light for your body. When your eye is healthy, your whole body is filled with light. But when your eye is unhealthy, your whole body is filled with darkness. And if the light you think you have is actually darkness, how deep that darkness is! No one can serve two masters.

> For you will hate one and love the other; you will be devoted to one and despise the other. You cannot serve God and be enslaved to money.
>
> — MATTHEW 6:21–24 NLT

* * *

### *Prayer of Encouragement*

*Thank You, God, for being a provider, strong tower, strength, mind regulator, comforter, shelter, and safe refuge. Abba Father, You are my Source. God, I thank You that You have everything I and my household need. I thank You for life and the very breath we breathe. I thank You for health and strength. I thank You for the activity of my limbs. I don't take it for granted. God, You are a good, good Father. You are so mindful of Your children.*

*I humbly ask, God, that if I or anyone in my household has sinned against thee, whether knowingly or unknowingly, that You would forgive us of our sins and cleanse us from all unrighteousness. We desire to live holy and righteous. Help us, God, to be kind and forgiving to others, just as You have forgiven us. Help us to bear with one another and to encourage one another to become all You desire for us to become in this earth. I thank You for providing every resource needed to live and for providing for my family and others.*

*Thank You, God, for a sound mind full of power and authority that You have given to me and my household. You provide everything we need. Help me to pull down every good and perfect gift You have for me. Help me to become a good steward of my financial matters.*

*Help me to inspect what I expect. God, I ask that Your Holy Spirit lead and guide me and my household daily. Holy Spirit, You are welcome to have Your way. God, open up my ears to hear and receive Your words and instructions.*

*Let change that You have purposed come within me and my household, and allow our hearts to receive this wisdom, knowledge, and understanding regarding taking ownership.*

*I decree and declare that stewardship over my financial matters will be prevalent in my life and my household for generations to come. I decree and declare that each member of my household will take You at Your word as they learn to become wise in their financial matters, and that they will teach each other these same instructions.*
*God, I thank You that Your covenant promises are Your assurance and Your guarantee to those who surrender to Your will and purpose. Thank You that Your Word cannot return to You void, but must accomplish the goal or assignment where it was intended. As I seek out Your Word and*

*meditate on Your promises, let it become a part of my daily life and lifestyle. As I seek, I shall find. As I knock, the doors will be opened, and as I ask, You shall supply every one of my needs according to Your riches in glory!*

*Bless me now, God, with good health, wealth, prosperity, abundance, and overflow. I love You, God. I adore You, and I and my household will give You our yes. Yes to Your will. Yes to Your ways. Yes, we will obey.*

*We cover these prayers and the unspoken prayers of my heart in the blood of Jesus. I call these prayers and the unspoken prayers already done.*

*In Jesus' mighty and matchless authority, we pray. Amen.*

> “Dishonest money dwindles away, but whoever gathers money little by little makes it grow.
>
> — PROVERBS 13:11 (NIV)

3

# INVESTMENT BLUNDERS TO AVOID (PART I)

> So God I put our trust in you. I put our hope in You, God.
>
> — NUMBERS 23:19 NLT

As we dive deeper into savings and investments, there are important things to note. There are several blunders to avoid when making investments for your retirement.

## What Are Blunders?

*Blunders* are careless mistakes. To make a blunder is to move or act blindly, stupidly, or without direction or steady guidance. It is also to make a gross or stupid mistake, especially through carelessness or mental confusion. A *mistake* is an act or judgment that is misguided or wrong or to be wrong about.

In my professional insight, there are five top blunders to avoid and become knowledgeable about before jumping into any savings/investment vehicle. Learn these techniques to prepare you and your household for great savings and investment returns.

Here are the top five blunders to avoid with detailed explanations for you and your family/household to discuss.

**Blunder #1: Placing Big Bets**

When placing a big bet, one must weigh the outcome. I know placing a big bet can be tempting, to say the least, especially when you feel that you have fallen behind on monthly responsibilities or borrowed against your retirement plan/savings. A good rule of thumb is to never make an investment decision from mixed emotions; never take someone's word without doing your due diligence in fact-finding (inspect what you expect). Be aware of potential scammers. They are very crafty, and deceitful, posing as professionals.

**Blunder #2: Being Too Conservative**

Conservative investing is an investment strategy that prioritizes the preservation of capital over growth and market returns. Preservation capital is a conservative investment strategy where you primarily focus on preserving capital and preventing loss in building a complete financial portfolio. This strategy necessitates investment in the safest short-term instruments such as treasury bills, certificates of deposit, fixed-income securities, money markets, and cash or cash equivalents.

*3 Key Points*

- Conservative investing prioritizes preserving the purchasing power of one's capital (income) with the least amount of risk.

- Conservative investing will most times include relatively high-weighting to low-risk securities.

- One looks more conservatively when there's a shortening in the time horizon (including older age), the need for current income over growth, or a view that asset prices will decline more quickly.

Remember the "life curve" from volume one *Art of Budgeting*? The life curve is volatile, meaning it's moving constantly, and if you are not wise, you will look up, and when it is time for retirement, you'll realize you have no savings or investments to fall back on. This curve starts with accumulation. When you begin working, you must also begin saving and investing in your future. Search out different avenues or instruments for saving. You learn with self-discipline to turn your income into assets. Assets equal liquid cash, cash on hand. At the top of the life curve, there is retirement. As consumers, we want our investments into real estate, stocks, bonds, dividends, 401(k), Certificates of Deposit (CDs), annuities, and individual retirement accounts (IRA) to work for us and provide liquid assets by retirement age.

On the downward side of the life curve, there is distribution. This is where your income has become assets, and it is now "working for you," meaning you are receiving "monthly dividend" disbursement from your investments. The investment is now paying you in monthly income, which adds to your gross monthly/ annual income, which directly affects your budget and buying power.

### Blunder #3: Falling for a Ponzi Scheme

A Ponzi scheme is a form of fraud that lures the investor (you or someone you may know) and pays profits to earlier investors with funds from more recent investors. The Ponzi was named after Italian businessman Charles Ponzi. He developed this scheme to lead suspecting victims to believe that profits will arrive from other legitimate business activity, such as product sales or successful investments. Investors remain unsuspecting that other investors are the source of the funds and as the majority do not demand full repayment and still believe in the nonexistent assets they are purported to own.

*Red Flags*

- High-Investment Returns with Little or No Risk: Any "guaranteed" investment opportunity should be considered suspect.

- Overly Consistent Returns: An investment that continues to generate regular positive returns regardless of overall market conditions is considered suspicious.

- Unregistered Investments: Registration with financial regulators like SEC (Securities and Exchange Commission) or FCA (Financial Conduct Authority) are important because they provide investors with access to key information about the company's management, products, services, and finances. The SEC and FCA enforce the law against market manipulation, plus maintain integrity of financial market.

- Unlicensed Sellers: In the United States, federal and state securities laws require that investment professionals and their firms be licensed or registered. Most Ponzi schemes are unregistered firms or individuals.

- Secretive or Complex Strategies: Investments that cannot be understood or on which no complete information can be found or obtained are considered suspicious.

- Issues with paperwork: A surefire red flag is account

statement errors, where funds are not being invested as promised.

- Difficulty Receiving Payment: Be very suspicious when you don't receive payment as promised or have difficulty cashing out. Promoters of a Ponzi scheme will often try to prevent participants from cashing out by offering a higher payout amount for staying put.

**Blunder #4: Paying Excess Fees**

A common mistake to avoid is paying excessive fees. Be sure to read the fine print. Fees cost you in two ways:

- Actual out-of-pocket expenses and charges
- The money you spend on fees is money that is not working for your benefit.

Be intentional about paying fees. The fees you may be paying could result in increased income when you stay on top of not paying excess fees.

**Blunder #5: Ignoring the Subtle Effects of Inflation**

Right now, all over the world, consumers are experiencing hyperinflation. Hyperinflation describes rapid, excess, and out-of-control general price increases in an economy. There are two common reasons for hyperinflation:

- *Excess Money Supply:* This happens mainly in times of great economic turmoil and depression. Economic depression, as we know, is an extended period of negative growth rate (two consecutive quarters of negative growth). The characteristics of hyperinflation are high unemployment, company and individual bankruptcies, lower productivity output, and less credit.

- *Loss of Confidence in the Economy or Monetary System:* This occurs when citizens lose confidence in their country's currency and the central banks' ability to maintain the currency value. This is very common during the times of war. Companies begin to request a risk premium for accepting money both within and outside the country. However, companies also raise their prices, creating hyperinflation. When currency is viewed as having little to no value, people (consumers) like you and me start hoarding items, especially valuable commodities. Cause and effect happens, and the price causes a scarcity of necessities like food and fuel. The government then releases money to bring about stability in pricing and create a liquidity problem.

### *Hyperinflation*

Have you all been to the grocery store recently? Prices have almost increased by 40–70%. On household items, I have experienced around a 40% increase. Be sure to include the increase in spending in your household weekly or monthly expense report (aka budget).

### *Inflation*

Inflation is sometimes classified into three types: demand-pull inflation, cost-push inflation, and built-in inflation. When prices rise, the ability to purchase multiple items decreases because one unit of money buys fewer goods and services. The loss of purchasing power impacts the cost of living for the common public, which ultimately leads to a deceleration in economic growth, money supply, and economic development.

Always take into consideration the inflation rate when

preparing your budget, planning for savings and investments, and building your complete financial portfolio.

As we move forward, I will be giving out some key nuggets for you to be informed and able to make sound strategic decisions regarding your investments in your retirement.

> Remember this—a farmer who plants only a few seeds will get a small crop. But the one who plants generously will get a generous crop. You must each decide in your heart how much to give. And don't give reluctantly or in response to pressure. For God loves a person who gives cheerfully. And God will generously provide all you need. Then you will always have everything you need and plenty left over to share with others.
>
> — 2 CORINTHIANS 9:6–8 NLT

* * *

***Prayer for Clarity***

*Father God, I come with a humble heart of thanksgiving, thanking You for Your goodness and mercy toward me and my household. We adore You, our sovereign God, our dependable God. We thank You for having food on our tables and food in our cabinets. I thank You for a roof over our heads and a bed to sleep in. I thank You for running water in our place of residence. I thank You for life and that life is more abundant.*

*You are King of kings and Lord over all. You are my strength when I am weak. You are my provider and my protector. Without You, God, where would I be? I thank You for stability and provision. For God, You promised that if I give to Your house, You would make sure that there is nothing lacking in my house, that I would overflow in abundance. Help me to give generously and be a cheerful giver to those in need as You have instructed me to be very mindful of widows, fatherless children, the poor, and the low in spirit.*

*We thank You for Malachi 3:10 (NLT), where it says, "Bring all the tithes into the storehouse so there will be enough food in my Temple. If You do, says the Lord of Heaven's Armies, I will open the windows of heaven for You. I will pour out a blessing so great You won't have enough room to take it in! Try it! Put me to the test!"*
*God is not a man, so he does not lie. He is not human, so he does not change his mind. Has he ever spoken and failed to act? Has he ever promised and not carried it through?*

*You will deliver all You promised if I would obey Your laws, commands, and instructions. Help me to repent, confess, and turn away from evil and wickedness— then to pray, seeking Your face earnestly. You are a good Father.*

*God, forgive me of any sins I may have committed, whether knowingly or unknowingly. God, help me to forgive others who have trespassed against me or those I hold near and dear to my heart. For You, give me the heart that enables me to forgive. Transform my heart, mind, body, and soul to put You first in everything I do, even down to the smallest of my daily existence.*

*Keep me in remembrance of Proverbs 22:7 (NLT): "Just as the rich rule the poor, so the borrower is servant to the lender." So on this day, God, I decree and declare that I am the head and not the tail. I am the lender and not the borrower. I am healthy and walking into my wealthy places. You are the God of miracles, signs, and wonders. I believe in Your power, and I believe in Your covenant promises. Now, God, let me down in Your Holy Spirit on this day. May Your presence fill this room and/or space.*

*Bestow upon my household knowledge, wisdom, understanding, and insight to increase in financial matters and creditworthiness. Give us clarity of thought and oneness in body, mind, and spirit. May everyone who reads this prayer, receive Your power and ability to create Kingdom wealth, God's way. Be ye, therefore, transformed by the renewing of our minds, Standing firmly and believing that we are not of this world or the world systems. We are God's chosen. Therefore, there is no lack in my household. "I have received God's Spirit (not the world's spirit), so I can know the wonderful things God has freely given" (1 Corinthians 2:12, NLT).*

*As I close this prayer, Father God, teach me to love unconditionally and forgive quickly, so that my prayers may not be hindered in any way. I cover these prayers and the unspoken prayers of my heart in the Blood of Jesus. I bind up the enemy's attack to try and steal this word of knowledge, and I release understanding, wisdom, and insight. I call it done right now.*

*In the matchless Name and Authority of Christ Jesus, we pray. Amen.*

# 4

# INVESTMENT BLUNDERS TO AVOID (PART II)

> Listen, I received a command to bless; God has blessed, and I cannot reverse it!
>
> — NUMBERS 23:20 NLT

I have some great financial tips and key nuggets for you to be informed and able to make sound strategic decisions regarding your investments in your retirement and savings expenditures. So we will jump right into securities, financial assets, stocks, derivatives, mutual funds, bonds, annuities, escrows, and dividends. These are income sources that you want to be knowledgeable and insightful of when taking a leap of faith in building and growing your household solidity.

Building a complete financial portfolio takes strategic planning. I will continue to provide biblical principles as well as wisdom, knowledge, understanding, and insight to achieve financial stability while building Kingdom wealth, God's way.

It's important that you start off the right way, but it's imperative that you end the right way. Here's a recap on building a complete financial portfolio as you and your household prepare to take ownership in every area of your life and lifestyle.

### *Recap*: What Is a Portfolio?

A portfolio is a range of investments held by a person or organization. It is a compilation of materials that exemplifies your beliefs, skills, qualifications, education, training, and experience. It provides insight into your personality and work ethic. It is also a grouping of financial assets such as stocks, bonds, commodities, currencies, and cash equivalents, as well as their fund counterparts, including mutual, exchange-traded, and closed funds. Portfolios are held by investors and/or managed by financial professionals and money managers.

### *Recap*: How Do You Build a Portfolio?

There are ten steps to build a complete financial portfolio:

1. Craft a balance sheet.
2. Contribute to your 401(k).
3. Pay off credit card debt and installment debt.
4. Open a Roth IRA.
5. Purchase a home.
6. Build six months' worth of emergency funds.
7. Look into other investments.
8. Invest in yourself.
9. Save for your children's education (empty nesters, save for your bucket list adventures).
10. Stay the course.

### Understanding Securities

Now, let's jump into our discussion about securities and define some common terms that are essential for your understanding.

- *Securities:* A security is a tradable financial asset of any kind. In the US, securities are broadly categorized into debt securities (e.g., banknotes, bonds, and debentures) and equity securities (e.g., common stocks).

- *Financial Assets:* These are usually more liquid than other tangible assets. These are property in law and are literally anything that can be touched, that includes both real property (land) and personal property (moveable property).

- *Debentures:* These are also called debt securities, which are medium- to long-term debt instruments used by large companies to borrow money at a fixed rate of interest. *Debentures* is the legal term originally referred to a document that either creates a debt or acknowledges it (e.g., banknotes or bonds).

- *Equity Securities (aka Stocks):* A single share of stock represents fractional ownership of the corporation in proportion to the total number of shares. This typically entitles you, the consumer or stockholder, to a fraction of the company's earnings, proceeds from liquidation of assets. Stocks can be bought and sold privately or on the stock exchanges, which are highly regulated by the government to prevent fraud, protect investors, and benefit the large economy.

Investing in securities involves a risk of loss. The past performance is never a guarantee of future returns. Investing in foreign stock markets involves additional risk, such as currency fluctuations (a change in an exchange rate). If a British pound is worth $2 on Monday and $1.80 on Tuesday, a somewhat dramatic currency fluctuation has occurred.

*Currency fluctuation* happens constantly and occurs for all floating currency (*floating currency* is a currency whose value is determined by the free market). *Floating currency* changes constantly, depending on the *supply and demand* for that currency as well as the amount of the currency held in foreign reserves. The advantage of a floating currency is that it tends to be more economically efficient. Lastly, a floating currency may undergo currency appreciation or currency depreciation, depending on the market fluctuations.

Nothing I am sharing with you today is intended to be a recommendation or a forecast of market conditions. Rather, I am illustrating a point. Current and future markets may differ significantly from those illustrated in the information shared.

Here are five key nuggets of wisdom that are essential for you to make sound strategic decisions regarding your investments in your retirement and savings expenditures.

### Wisdom Nugget #1: Stock Options

Stock options issued by many companies as part of their employee compensation plans do not represent ownership, but represent the right to buy ownership at a future time at a specified price.

- *Derivatives:* In the finance world, a derivative is a contract that derives its value from the performance of an underlying entity. This underlying entity can be an asset, a value of ownership that can convert to cash.

- *Index:* This is a mutual fund and is an open-end professionally managed investment fund that pools money from many investors to purchase securities.

- *Mutual Funds Advantages (Economic Scale/ Microeconomics):* These are the cost advantages that an enterprise obtains due to their scale of operations with cost per unit of output decreasing with increasing scale.

- *Microeconomics:* This is a branch of economics that studies the behavior of individuals and firms in making decisions regarding the allocation of *scarce resources* and the interactions among these individuals and firms.

- *Scarcity:* This is the limited availability of a commodity, which may be in demand in the market or by the commons. Scarcity also includes an individual's lack of resources to buy commodities. The opposite of scarcity is *abundance.*

- *Diversification.* This is the process of a company enlarging or varying its range of products or field of operations (always compare and explore other markets for the best products).

- *Liquidity:* This is the availability of liquid assets to a market or company and/or an individual consumer.

- *Professional Management:* This means the company has professional administrative and technical skills qualifications and also a good amount of experience in managing business affairs.

Keep in mind that *mutual funds* come with fees and expenses.

Here's some important information to consider:

- *Disadvantages of Mutual Funds:* These charges may be incurred by investors (you) who hold mutual funds.

- *Cost:* Value of money that has been used to produce something or deliver a service, and hence is not available for use anymore.

- *Investment:* To allocate more in expectation of some benefit in the future.

- *Fees:* The price we pay as investors for the right of service.

- *Marketing:* The study and management of exchanged relationships. This is also the process of identifying, anticipating, and satisfying consumer needs and wants. It's used to attract consumers, the primary components of business management and commerce.

- Often called the underlying of a *derivative* is an asset, or a basket of assets (a group of several securities created for the purpose of simultaneous buying and selling). An underlying may be a price or rate of an asset or liability, but is not the asset or liability.

- *Index Funds:* A basket for all the securities in a particular exchange, weighted appropriately.

**Wisdom Nugget #2: Index**

In economics and finance, an index is a statistical measure of change in a representative group of individual data points, or even another derivative, such that the cash flow of the (former) derivative depend on the value of this underlying. There must be an independent way to observe this value to avoid conflicts of interest.

*1. Bonds*: An instrument of indebtedness of the bond issuer to the holders, which is you, the consumer. The most common types of bonds are the following:

- *Municipal Bonds*: Commonly known as a muni bond. A muni bond is a bond issued by a local government or territory or one of their agencies (e.g., public projects such as roads, schools, airports, seaports, and infrastructure-related repairs).

- *Corporate Bonds:* A bond issued by a corporation in order to raise financing for a variety of reasons, such as operations, mergers and acquisitions, or to expand business.

Thus, a bond is a form of a loan or IOU. The holder of the bond is the lender (creditor), the issuer of the bond is the borrower (debtor), and the coupon is the interest.

Bonds provide the borrower with external funds to finance long-term investments or, in the case of government bonds, to finance current expenditures (certificates of deposit or short-term commercial paper are considered to be money market instruments and not bonds; the main difference is the length of the term of the instruments).

Bonds and stocks are both securities. When investing, let's keep this in mind:

*Escrows + Dividends = Income*

2. *Escrow:* A bond, deed, or other document kept in the custody of a third party and taking effect only when a specified condition has been fulfilled. In North America, it is to be placed in custody or in a trust. Now, in layman's terms, this means an escrow service is basically a middleman between a buyer and a seller, or in the case of a mortgage, a middleman between a homeowner and the county (for property taxes), insurance companies, and anyone else who the homeowner designates to pay with funds from the escrow account.

3. *Dividends:* A sum of money paid regularly (typically quarterly) by a company to its shareholders out of its profits (or reserves). When a corporation earns a profit or surplus, the corporation is able to reinvest the profit in the business

(called retained earnings) and pay a proportion of the profit as a dividend to shareholders.

*Dividend Income* refers to any distribution of a company's earnings to shareholders from stocks or mutual funds you own. The tax treatment of dividend income depends on whether the income meets the definition of a "qualified dividend," and if it is held in a retirement account, like an IRA (individual retirement account), it is considered a qualified dividend.

**Wisdom Nugget #3: IRA**

An IRA functions mostly like a certificate of deposits instrument (CD), wherein funds are deposited over a period of time. The longer you invest, the more interest that will be paid to you the consumer. After age fifty-nine and a half, you are required to take minimum distribution payments once a year until age seventy and a half.

- *Consider a Roth IRA:* A Roth IRA is an individual retirement account allowing a person to set aside after-tax income up to a specified amount each year. Both earnings on the account and withdrawals after the age of fifty-nine and a half are tax-free.

- *Note:* If you continue working, no required distribution is mandatory.

**Wisdom Nugget # 4: 403(b) Plan**

A 403(b) Plan is like a 401(k) for educators and nonprofit employees, and can help supplement your pension or other retirement savings. It's specifically designed for education and nonprofit professionals, and it has the flexibility to adjust as your needs change and can help you turn your salary into a more comfortable retirement.

*Features and Benefits of 403(b) Plans:*

- *Every dollar counts.* You can increase or decrease deposit contributions up to the federal maximum at any time.

- *It's automatic.* You pay yourself first because it's deducted right from your paycheck.

- *It's flexible.* You can select the investment you're most comfortable with and change them when you want.

- *You won't pay taxes while you're saving.* Your taxes are deferred until you withdraw the money from your account, which is typically when you're retired and in a lower tax bracket. That means all your earnings stay invested, letting your money grow faster than it would in a taxable account.

*College Savings:*

- *Highly rated 529 College Savings Plan:* With this Bright Start Plan, you and your household can benefit from all of the attractive benefits that have earned the Bright Start back-to-back-to-back gold medals from Morningstar. Bright Start is flexible. The money in your account can be used to pay qualified higher-education expenses at any eligible school— college, university, vocational, trade, or graduate— anywhere in the United States and even some abroad. Check out the listing of eligible schools from the Department of Education website.

- *Great tax benefits:* Bright Start provides excellent tax benefits, including tax-deferred growth of any earnings while in the plan, along with tax-free withdrawals for qualified college expenses. Contribution is $15K per year/per child ($30K for married couples) for tax advantages.

- *Low cost:* Bright Start has some of the lowest costs of any 529 Plan. Accounts can be opened by almost anyone, including individuals, UGMA/UTMA (Uniform Gift to Minors Act and the Uniform Transfer to Minors Act accounts), custodians, certain legal entities, or a trust. These accounts let investors (you) take advantage of the lower tax rate for children while saving for education. Even if you're unsure if your beneficiary will attend college, these UGMA/UTMA accounts aren't limited to education expenses. Withdrawals can be used for anything that benefits the beneficiary. The age transfer of these accounts is eighteen or twenty-one in most states —the beneficiary is entitled to the account. Keep in mind that there are no contribution limits on UGMA/UTMA accounts.

### Wisdom Nugget #5: Annuities

Annuities are a form of insurance or investment entitling the investor to a series of annual sums. Annuities are a fixed sum of money paid to someone each year, typically for the rest of their life, with growth potential. A good rule of thumb when purchasing annuities is to always pay close attention to the fee schedule and/or penalties. Another important component is to check for survivor benefits. Inspect what you expect to ensure that what you leave behind for surviving spouse or beneficiary will be a sustainable amount for their life expectancy.

### Take Action

You can go to protectedincome.org to download worksheets and checklists to prepare to speak with your financial professional/money manager.

I would love to be your accountability coach to help you and your household navigate the savings and investment entities that we have discussed thus far. You can go to my website: www.trifoldconnectionsllc.com, email me at: info@trifoldconnectionsllc.com, or call me at: 708-553-0002 to make an appointment. Your initial consultation is free. My website is user-friendly. Share with a friend or loved one, as sharing is caring; caring is showing love, which is something this world can truly afford more of.

* * *

***Prayer of Acknowledgement***

*God of miracles, signs, and wonders, I will take You at Your Word and trust You completely. Increase my faith to believe what I do not see. Surround me and my household with Your peace that surpasses all our understanding. Give us wisdom.*

*Open up our minds to receive understanding about our financial matters. Help us to become better money managers. Help me and my family to invest in our future. Let our faith be bigger than our fear!*

*I love You! I thank You. We are blessed in every way because You are with me and my household.*

*In Jesus' Mighty Name, we pray. Amen.*

* * *

# 5

# RETIREMENT PLANNING MISTAKES TO AVOID

> Get all the advice and instruction you can, so you will be wise the rest of your life.
>
> — PROVERBS 19:20 NLT

When deciding to start planning for retirement, you must weigh the risks and fees associated with every plan you inquire about. The earlier you start investing in yourself, the greater the return. The overall goal is to provide additional income to your monthly/annual household income. Let us now look into more extenuating circumstances surrounding savings and investments and planning for retirement.

> But you must remain faithful to the things you have been taught. You know they are true, for you know you can trust those who taught you. You have been taught the holy Scriptures from childhood, and they have given you the wisdom to receive salvation that comes by trusting in Christ Jesus. All Scripture is inspired by God and is useful to teach us what is true

> and to make us realize what is wrong in our lives. It corrects us when we are wrong and teaches us to do what is right. God uses it to prepare and equip his people to do every good work.
>
> — 2 TIMOTHY 3:14–17 NLT

**Mistake #1: Setting Improper Goals**

Many investment managers focus exclusively on areas such as risk tolerance. While this is a very important factor to consider, it's also important to build a complete financial portfolio that addresses your overall goals.

You should know the overall goal you want to reach with your portfolio's intended use. You must ask questions like "Will I need cash flow to fund retirement expenses, or growth, so you can leave money to your beneficiaries or charities of choice? Or both?"

Without a detailed understanding of your goals and being unable to focus on how to achieve these goals, you may find that you are unable to maintain the lifestyle you desire or worst-case scenario, you may possibly run out of money in your retirement.

*How to Avoid This Mistake*

Defining your goals should be your first order of business in the investment and savings process. Most goals are centered on the need for cash flow, growth, or a combination of the two. After you define how you want your portfolio to work for you and the expected changes over time, it's important to establish your investment "life curve" or your "life expectancy" and who will be your beneficiaries. Knowing how long your portfolios need to last is important, as well as determining your asset allocation—the mix of stocks, bonds, cash, and other securities in your portfolio.

Here at Tri Fold Connections, we desire to help you with your short-term and long-term financial goals and help you create a plan and stick to it, partnering with you to ensure that your savings and investment goals remain consistent with your plan for retirement. If you decide to change your savings and investment instruments, we will work with you to see that the changes are made, and everything is updated successfully.

### Mistake #2: Underestimating the Life Curve for Your Assets

The life curve, simply put, is the length of time you expect to work and accumulate income, build for retirement, and then have those distributed to you over your life expectancy. This is also called time horizon. So again, one must plan and set goals and objectives to achieve the desired savings and investments for your retirement. Keep in mind that one must also include one's beneficiaries' life expectancy in our equations.

*How to Avoid This Mistake*

The life curve and time horizon are unique to each individual investor and are often longer than life expectancy. Start savings and investment instruments early in your career or employment.

Our goal at Tri Fold Connections is to help you understand your specific financial needs, both today and for your future, helping you to achieve the legacy you would like to leave on earth. We educate our clients that making decisions from their emotions regarding asset allocations could result in running out of cash flow for their retirement needs.

### Mistake #3: Ignoring the Impact of Inflation on Your Portfolio

A common mistake that some industry professionals miss the mark is on the nominal dollar value of your portfolio without considering purchasing power. Over time, our portfolio's purchasing power can diminish due to inflation. As prices of items increase, oftentimes today's dollar will buy less in the future. Inflation's negative impact on our purchasing power means we need more portfolio growth than we originally anticipated.

For example, food prices have increased since the COVID-19 outbreak in March 2020; hospital services, medical care, prescription drugs, housing, cars, fuel, and more have increased. Therefore, we must not just focus on short-term goals but plan accordingly for our long-term financial needs that will be able to sustain us and our purchasing power over the long haul.

### *How to Avoid This Mistake*

We need to consider inflation and how to grow our purchasing power as well as the dollar value of our portfolio. When considering our investments returns, it is critical to include the impact of inflation in today's society. Inflation on average increases 3% per year; we can just say our portfolio may have a growth of 5% annually, but we only see a 2% increase annually due to inflation being 3%. That's not much growth in our purchasing power.

At Tri Fold Connections, we take inflation into considerable account when we analyze your current portfolio and make recommendations based on an optimal asset allocation to achieve your goals.

## **Mistake #4: Incompletely Judging Investment Risk**

The industry oftentimes judges the investment risk incorrectly. Investors and advisers alike have made these types of mistakes, having an incomplete view of investment risk. Many believe risk only exists in a short-term volatility markets. Another significant risk is that of not achieving your long-term investing goals. For example, some investors load their portfolios with low-yielding US treasury bonds to avoid stock market volatility—even though their investment time horizons and life curve expectancy is more than twenty or thirty years out. This strategy typically offers a lack in quantity and/or quality of our investments, especially when we consider inflation, which can put us into significant risk of not reaching our long-term goals.

*How to Avoid This Mistake*

Generally, the longer our time horizon or life expectancy is, the more our short-term volatility we may need to bear, depending on our cash flow needs and return objectives. The short-term volatility, which means easily evaporated or liable to change rapidly and unpredictably, usually for the worst, that is inherent in stocks can make us feel uneasy about investing, but stocks are much more likely to help our portfolio's growth over the long haul. Keep this in mind, stocks have outperformed bonds in 97% of the twenty-year periods since 1926. When stocks outperform bonds over twenty-year periods, it tends to be a wide margin. When bonds outperform stocks, the outperformance tends to be far greater and modest.

Tri Fold Connections would love to help you understand your exposure to investment risk as well as your life curve and time horizon and investment objectives in order to recommend an optimal "complete financial portfolio" and asset allocations.

**Mistake #5: Hiring a Fiduciary Who Doesn't Act in Your Best Interest**

We must be aware of the financial planners/advisers we hire to analyze our financial portfolios. Always look for a financial planner/adviser with integrity.

*How to Avoid This Mistake*

When meeting with this planner/adviser, you should:

- Ask open-ended questions to engage them in revealing their honesty, moral principles, and moral uprightness

- Ask about their values. Values guide actions, and an adviser's values should always include putting their client's best interest first.

- Ask about their philosophy in savings and investment.

- Ask about is their source of compensation and any potential conflicts of interest. You want to know their fee schedule up front. If you hire an adviser who sells commission-based products or values their bottom line over your goals as the client, they may not always serve your needs or act in your best interest.

**Mistake #6: Paying Too Much in Fees**

Even healthy savings and investments returns can be undermined by hidden fees. Overall, trading costs have decreased over time with better technology and increased market liquidity, but layers of fees can still add up and decrease your potential profitable income. In some cases, fees can make or break your ability to reach your overall savings and investment goals.

*How to Avoid This Mistake*

Make sure you know the planner's/adviser's fee structure and what, if any, incentives they may receive for them to act in your best interest.

Tri Fold Connections' philosophy and fee structure are driven by acting in the best interest of our clients. We are a fee-only planner/adviser and do not earn commissions from trading in your account. We are intentional about assisting you in savings and investments to help build and manage your portfolios, assisting you with planning for retirement, and helping you also to deal with adverse credit. Our simple and transparent fee schedule is based on our clients' affordability of our services. We also work with you in order to assist and help provide informative directions of products and or services providing transparency to instill your trust.

Our main objective is to help you grow exponentially, growing you rapidly to achieve your overall long-term goals. We believe that good advice focuses on your short-term and long-term goals and your best interests.

### Mistake #7: Confusing Income Needs with Cash Flow Needs

To avoid this problem, let's define these two terms. *Cash flow* is the money that you will need for your living expenses and other personal needs. *Income* is money received from a portfolio, such as equity dividends and fixed-income interest. Now the difference between the two is very important. The way in which you generate income can have a tangible effect (i.e., touch) on the growth of your assets as well as on the amount of taxes you pay. Both have a direct impact on your ability to achieve your required cash flow.

Tri Fold Connections starts by gaining a full understanding of your cash flow needs and expected income and expenses. Once we have defined your goals and objectives, we can estimate the likelihood of your assets and recommend a savings and investments plan according to your needs.

### Mistake 8: Relying on Annuities for Safe Growth

One of the biggest risks we face as investors is running out of money after we have retired. Some brokers and financial planners will pitch annuities as "safe" products that boost "guaranteed withdrawals" or "minimum returns" in an effort to appease our fears. Some annuities can be very costly, complex investment vehicles with hidden fee schedules that can cost us the investor up to 3.44% annually when factoring in optional riders! (Riders is an add-on cover to the base annuity that has additional fees' premiums attached.) Now, other annuities may advertise no fees, but you may have difficulties understanding their performance calculations that greatly water down your returns on your investments. These investments may have some severe restrictions that could offset your potential benefits.

Tri Fold Connections does not sell annuities. We seek to educate our clients about the complexities surrounding annuities to help you determine if purchasing different types of annuities is an appropriate investment given your financial goals. Tri Fold Connections does not earn commissions from selling products; we offer you our professional service, and we have a fair and transparent fee structure that aligns our interest with your interests, goals, and values. You can scan the QR code in the front of this book, or you can visit us at: www.trifoldconnectionsllc.com

> So teach us to number our days, That we may cultivate and bring to You a heart of wisdom.
>
> — PSALM 90:12 AMP

> If any of you lacks wisdom [to guide him thorough a decision or circumstance], he is to ask of [our benevolent] God, who gives to everyone generously and without rebuke or blame, and it will be given to him.
>
> —JAMES 1:5 AMP

> Teacher, which is the most important commandment in the law of Moses? Jesus replied, 'You must love the LORD your God with all your heart, all your soul, and all your mind.' This is the first and greatest commandment. A second is equally important: 'Love your neighbor as yourself.'
>
> — MATTHEW 22:36–39 NLT

* * *

### *Prayer of Courage*

*Gracious Father, we come before You today to say thank You. We adore You, God, You are the Great I AM. Wonderful Counselor, the King of kings, the Lord of lords, mighty in battle, Jehovah Shalom our peace, Jehovah Jireh Our Provider.*

*Father God, if we have committed any sin against You or our brother or sister of omission or commission, we ask for forgiveness God. We desire to have a clean heart and renew a right spirit within us.*

*Thank You, God, for keeping us all week long. Thank You for protecting our residence. Thank You, God, for safety as we travel to work, appointments, and our leisure activities. Thank You, God, that You keep our children safe as they travel to and fro. Thank You, God, that we have food to eat, clothes to wear, shoes on our feet. Thank You, God, that we have a bed to sleep in. Thank You, God, that You take care of us day in and day out. Thank You, God, that You never grow weary. We thank You, God, for our health and our strength. We thank You, God, for the activity of our limbs, that we can move and have our very being. We thank You, God, for the ability to make sound decisions and stick to our plans. We thank You for supernatural debt cancellation. We thank You that we are exercising self-discipline and self-control in all areas of our lives, specifically in our finances.*

*Help us to become good stewards of our financial resources. Help us to grow in faith, believing, trusting, and obeying Your precepts. Let our faith be BIGGER than our fear. We thank You for an accountability partner, a person who will be diligent and help us reach our goals. Help us to seek wise counsel, godly counsel. We place our plans before You, God, for You are the chief executive officer, and we know You have our best interest at heart.*

*Now, God, we ask that You blow a fresh wind on our goals, dreams, assignments, and vision. Father, give us the courage to step out of the familiar and explore new avenues. Give us the courage to take a leap of faith, the courage to be wise investors. Without You, we would fail. With You, all things are possible. What seems impossible to us is possible with You as the head of our life. We thank You in advance that we can speak a word that can change the trajectory of our life, according to our faith.*

*I ask for blessings and an overflow of blessings to every person's household who is reading this book and learning how to take ownership, take possession or repossession, accountability, responsibility, and exercise self-discipline and self-control in every area of their life and lifestyle. We thank You in advance that as we set our goals, dreams, assignments, and visions before You in this decade, we will look back at our journals and see the manifestations of Your promises.*

*Now, God, help us to be debt-free—free from any bondages holding us back from the blessings that You have in store for all of us. We bind up the enemies' attack to try and come and steal this word of knowledge. We bind any retaliatory demon and cast them back to the pits of hell from whence they came. We seal these prayers and the unspoken prayers of our hearts in Jesus's blood and His righteousness.*

*In the matchless Name of Jesus, we pray. Amen.*

> “The righteous will flourish like a palm tree, they will grow like a cedar of Lebanon; planted in the house of the Lord, they will flourish in the courts of our God. They will still bear fruit in old age, they will stay fresh and green, proclaiming, 'The Lord is upright; he is my Rock, and there is no wickedness in him.
>
> — PSALM 92:12-15 (NIV)

CREDIT

# 6

# CREDIT 101 (PART I)

> And every one that was in distress, and every one that was in debt, and every one that was discontented, gathered themselves unto him; and he became a captain over them: and there were with him about four hundred men.
>
> — 1 SAMUEL 22:2 KJV

In this chapter, you will learn how to properly read your credit report. It's imperative that we all become very familiar with our history. Credit is one report that will go back in our history to tell a story of our capability to be accountable and responsible for our past financial matters as well as the ability to pay off our existing debt. It is our responsibility to ensure that this information is correct and accurate. Checking your credit report and FICO score once a year is a must. Let us now explore how to properly read your credit report.

## Four Main Sections of the Credit Report

The four main sections of the credit report are: personal information, credit history, public record, and credit inquiries. This section explains each of the four areas in greater detail.

### *Personal Information*

This section contains your name, address (past and present), Social Security number, date of birth, and names you may have used in the past. You want this section to be as accurate as possible. If you find any discrepancies in your name, address, phone number, Social Security number, date of birth, or maiden names/surnames, file a report immediately with all three credit bureaus for the corrections to be made within a sixty-day (60-day) period. The credit report agencies have sixty (60) days to respond and correct the discrepancies. Normally, they will inform you of their decision by mail.

### *Credit History*

Here you'll find a list of credit accounts, both open and closed, as well as payment information. If you have unused or unnecessary credit cards, you may want to reevaluate the value of those accounts.

You want to check this section of your credit report with a fine-tooth comb. Why? This section should reflect your personal indebtedness or accounts that you have paid in full and still remain open for the history to reflect longevity and your excellent payment history. Also, if you have accounts you no longer need that are fairly new, you may decide to close these accounts. When you close an account, your credit score will decrease, and within sixty days, it will increase again. Lastly, any credit that you have held in excellence for a long period of time should remain open on your credit report regardless of whether it's paid in full or not. If you close these accounts, it will wipe away all your credit history.

### *Public Record*

Information from collection agencies appears in this section, including judgments, delinquent accounts, bankruptcies, foreclosures, lawsuits, tax liens, and the like.

This section is critical. Before you can be approved for a mortgage, student loan, credit card, etc., these public records must be either paid in full, a payment plan in place (with first-month installment up front), a settlement agreement, and a letter from the lien holder stating the terms of the agreement. Now, if the lien holder, creditor, or collection agency decides to settle, once the settlement is received, they will issue a letter of payment in full or the settlement agreement terms and/or remove adverse credit reporting from your public record. It's important that when you communicate with these entities you keep good records. Record the date, times, who you spoke with, from what department, details discussed, and any agreement reached, and be sure to get an email address and/or contact phone number, with the best time to follow up if you have more questions.

### *Credit Inquires*

In this section, you'll find a list of everyone who has asked to see your credit report in the last two years for hard and soft inquiries.

A hard inquiry, also known as a hard pull, typically happens when a creditor checks your credit for the purpose of giving you a loan or credit card. Hard inquiries can potentially drop your credit scores, and they can result in your paying higher interest rates and fees for loans and revolving credit.

According to FICO, a hard inquiry will typically result in a 5–10 point drop in your credit scores. Hard inquiries remain on your credit report for two years, but usually only impact your credit score for a few months, not more than twelve months. Applying for credit can knock a few points off your credit score as well.

Credit inquiries remain visible on your credit report for two years, and studies have shown that people with six or more inquiries on their report are eight times more likely to default on their loans.

### How Can You Get Credit Inquiries Removed?

One way is to go directly to the creditor by sending a certified letter in the mail. In your letter, be sure to point out which inquiry (or inquiries) were not authorized, and then request those inquiries to be removed. Secondly, contact the three big credit bureaus where the unauthorized inquiry has shown up (Equifax, Experian, TransUnion).

The credit bureaus have up to sixty days to comply with your request in writing and supply you with an updated credit report showing the inquiry has been removed.

### How Does a Soft Inquiry Work?

There are several ways in which a soft inquiry can take place:

- You can check your own credit report.
- One of your current creditors can check your credit for validity or a credit line increase.
- You can apply for a soft pull pre-approval with a creditor.
- A company can check your credit to see if you qualify for pre-approval offers.

Soft inquiries can appear in their own section on your credit report. Also, remember that the three credit bureaus could have different inquiries, as an inquiry is only added to the credit report that was pulled. For example, if you only checked Experian, the soft inquiry won't be added to Equifax or TransUnion credit reports.

Credit scoring models generate your credit score by analyzing the information in your credit report. Soft inquiries do not have an impact on your credit scores.

**Building Your Credit Score**

To build your credit score, consider checking your credit score and if you have any late or missed payments.

*When to Check Your Credit?*

Check your credit score 120 days prior to applying for a mortgage loan, refinance, home equity loan, student loan, credit card, etc. to potentially correct any problems that are incorrect or fraudulent.

*Late or Missed Payments*

If you have negative marks on your credit report, pay any delinquencies and ask furnishers to remove inaccurate information. Wait to have at least six months of current payments before applying for a mortgage, refinance, home equity loan, student loan, and the like. The older a delinquency, the better your credit looks.

**Thin Credit History**

If you have a thin credit history, there are several things you can do to build it up.

- Consider adding one or two revolving credit cards.
- Pay your bill on time monthly.
- Your cell phone bill, energy bill, and gas bill can be used as a form of unconventional credit history.

The more you understand how credit works, the more confident you will feel about your financial decisions.

> "Trust in the Lord with all your heart; do not depend on your own understanding. Seek his will in all you

> do, and he will show you which path to take. Don't be impressed with your own wisdom. Instead, fear the Lord and turn away from evil. Then you will have healing for your body and strength for your bones.
>
> Honor the Lord with your wealth and with the best part of everything you produce. Then he will fill your barns with grain, and your vats will overflow with good wine.
>
> My child, don't reject the Lord's discipline, and don't be upset when he corrects you. For the Lord corrects those he loves, just as a father corrects a child in whom he delights.
>
> — PROVERBS 3:5–12 NLT

* * *

***Prayer of Ownership***

*Father God, we humble ourselves before You to say thank You. Thank You for a sound mind, a mind that can make strategic decisions, decisions that will catapult us to living a debt-free life, living in the freedom that Your words promises us. Thank You that we shall be obedient to Your will and Your word. Thank You that Your anger only lasts a moment. Thank You for forgiveness.*

*Father God, if we have done anything to sin against thee or our sisters or brothers, knowingly or unknowingly, we humbly beg for Your forgiveness. You said in Your word that we must love our neighbor as much as we love ourselves. We must also forgive and release the debts of those who have hurt, deceived, manipulated, or taken us for granted. Help us in our unforgiveness, realizing that we must love even our enemies as ourselves. Pray for those who have despitefully used us. Hate the sin and not the sinner.*

*For God, You desire for none of Your children to be lost or miss out on salvation and eternal life. Father God, we know that obedience is better than sacrifice. Help us to be radically obedient to Your word and follow Your precepts. God, Your word promises us that You give us the ability to create wealth. Help us to be seated before people who will give us wise council, those who are willing to take the initiative to help us create a strategy intended to resolve a difficulty or improve a situation, a fresh approach to our new skills. Help us to take action in resolving our debt and credit issues. Help us to complete a budget and balance sheet to allow us a visual account of our spending habits. Help us to start saving and investing in our future. Help us to take possessions and ownership of all the things You have promised us by faith believing that You can do just what You said.*

*Father God, help us to trust You and the accountability coach You have before us. We thank You for Your wisdom, knowledge, and understanding. We thank You that we are becoming good stewards of our financial matters.*

*In Jesus' Mighty Authority, we pray. Amen.*

CREDIT

# 7

# CREDIT 101 (PART II)

> God bought you for a price; so do not become slaves of human beings.
>
> — 1 CORINTHIANS 7:23 GNB

In the previous chapter, we discussed the four main sections on your credit report. Let's briefly review:

1. Personal Information
2. Credit History
3. Public Records
4. Credit Inquiries

We have covered some good ground and important information regarding our credit reports and the reporting credit agencies, including God's opinion regarding our debt. The Bible leaves no doubt about God's opinion regarding our debt.

> Owe no one nothing except to love one another; for he who loves his neighbor has fulfilled the law.
>
> — ROMANS 13:8 NLT

> The rich rules over the poor, and the borrower becomes the lender's slave.
>
> — PROVERBS 22:7 NIV

In our world today, many people have ignored these very truths. In the United States alone, hundreds of thousands of people are on the brink of bankruptcy. Millions of people are not only living paycheck to paycheck, but they're also living within sixty days of being homeless or in dire straits due to their finances and financial resources.

A national deficit occurs when the money going out exceeds the money coming in for a given period of time. Fiscal year to date (since October 2022) total updated monthly using the monthly treasury statement (MTS) dataset. Compared to the national deficit of $668 billion for the same period last year (October 2021–March 2022), our national deficit has increased by $432 billion, according to www.fiscaldata.treasury.gov. The federal government ran a deficit of $378 billion in March 2023, a $185 billion change from the deficit of $193 billion that was recorded in March 2022. Spending is up by $184 billion relative to last year, and revenues fell by $2 billion, according to www.pgpf.org.

The largest increases in spending occurred for the Department of Education ($35 billion) as a part of the pause on student loan repayment and spending by the Federal Deposit Insurance Corporation ($29 billion) stemming from two bank failures. Other categories that saw spending grow by more than $10 billion compared with March 2022 are Medicare, interest on the public debt, Department of Defense, Veterans Benefits and Services, and Social Security. On the revenue side, income and payroll taxes rose by $13 billion, a decrease in remittances from the Federal Reserve.

The national debt is costing Americans, higher interest rates. The interest adds up fast. As the debt grows, so does the interest we pay as consumers. Similar to purchasing a home or car loan, interest payments represent the price we pay to borrow money. As we borrow more and more, federal interest costs rise higher and compound over time. Rapidly growing interest payments are a burden that hinders our future economy.

The national debt matters because it affects our future and the future generations to come. We must make a conscious effort to build and leave a better future for our children and their children. Being irresponsible with our budget is simply not fair to our children and our grandchildren, who will be the ones to inherit our debt.

We have brought into a "buy now, pay later" philosophy of the world's systems, which has been sold to us for decades by advertisements tempting us to believe we must have this product or service that they are selling in order for us to project an image of self-worth. In short, we have been swallowing and digesting the lies of this world and its systems. As we try to digest the world system on debt, it causes us to regurgitate the awful lies that it's been selling us for decades.

God does not want us in debt. The only thing that we are to owe one another is love, which we are to give freely and in generous forms. We're to be givers, not borrowers. The price we pay for indebtedness can be extremely high.

In ancient times, we have all heard about the Israelites. They lost most of their land and possessions because of debt, and some sold themselves or their children into slavery in order to pay off debts (Nehemiah 5:3–5). We may have strong feelings of disbelief or even disappointment. How horrific for one to sell their own flesh and blood to pay off a debt. Yet, that's exactly what many are doing in this day and time, leaving our children with an unsurmountable amount of debt long after we are gone.

Additionally, God does not want His people in debt because it has a negative impact on our spiritual lives. Some of the reasons God is opposed to debt can be noticed when we take a look at the reason we take on debt in the first place. Many of us fall into debt traps:

- We buy things we can't afford.
- We make unwise investments.
- We get careless in our purchases, making unwise or even unnecessary choices.
- We don't look at the related cost in the future.
- We may lose our jobs or miss work due to an illness, injury, or just laziness.

Let's take this nugget away with us today. It's far easier to *stay* out of debt than it is to *get* out of debt. We must make a conscious decision to follow God's plan for our finances and guard against falling into the world systems of the alluring messages that tempt us to borrow and buy beyond our means or spend our money unwisely.

Proverbs 13:22 (MSG) reminds us, "A good man leaveth an inheritance to his children's children: and the wealth of the sinner is laid up for the just." It says a good life gets passed on to the grand-children, and ill-gotten wealth ends up with good people.

### What Your Credit Score Means

A credit score is typically a three-digit number based on information in your credit report that measures your risk level to the lenders. It's usually calculated using these five categories: payment history, amounts owed, length of credit history, types of credit in use, and new credit, which can always change. That's the good news if your credit scores are on the low side; you can take the necessary steps to improve your scores. The opposite is true if your credit scores are on the high side of the scale. A few slip-ups could potentially knock your scores down a notch or tremendously. Your scores can vary depending on the information available, so they could vary from credit bureau to credit bureau. The three major reporting agencies are Equifax, Experian, and TransUnion.

Our scores are divided into five categories:

1. Payment History - 35%
2. Amounts Owed- 30%
3. Length of Credit History - 15%
4. Types of Credit in Use - 10%
5. New Credit - 10%

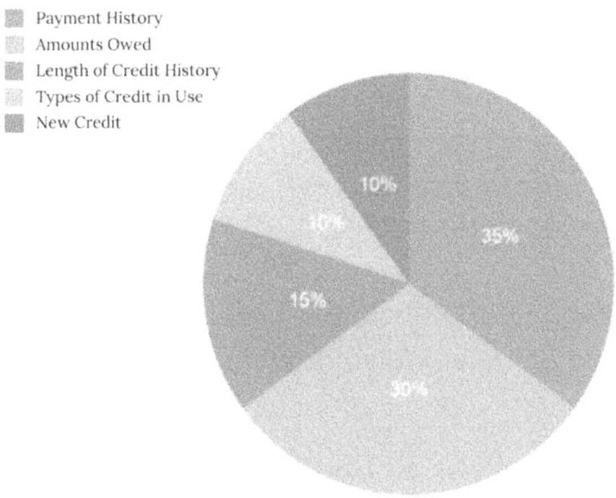


This chart reveals to us how our credit is weighed. Your payment history is the most important, with credit limits running a close second. Thirdly, the length of time you have a creditor is key when the underwriter is reviewing your loan for approval.

**How to Boost Your Credit Score**

Here are a few credit-related habits to help you improve your credit score:

- **Do**: Keep your balances manageable and under your credit limit.
- **Don't**: Exceed your limits on your credit card accounts.

- **Do:** Make your credit payments on time every month, including loans, utilities, and mortgage payments.
- **Don't:** Miss a credit payment or fail to pay at least the minimum amount due

- **Do:** Keep credit accounts that you have historically paid on time.
- **Don't:** Apply for a lot of credit accounts in a short amount of time.

- **Do:** Check your credit report once a year for accurate information being reported.
- **Don't:** File for bankruptcy or get your credit account turned over to a collection agency.

Avoid late payments. Set up payment reminders with your accounts so you never accidentally miss a due date.

### Does Carrying a Balance on Your Credit Card Hurt Your Credit Score?

Carrying a balance on your credit card can hurt your credit score if the balance gets too high. Your credit score is influenced by how much available credit you have and the balances you owe on both revolving and installment accounts. Revolving accounts usually means an open line of credit that can be used as needed up to a certain limit—like a credit card—rather than an installment loan that's taken out all at once, and then paid back over a fixed schedule. Some examples are mortgages, car loans, and purchases of furniture/appliances.

One advantage of a revolving account is convenience. Even if you pay it off, it stays open, so this way you can use it again if you need it without having to apply for additional credit or a credit line increase. Revolving accounts are beneficial to have on your credit reports because over time, they show a history of how well you have managed your credit. It's ideal to have some revolving accounts, as well as some installment accounts with fixed monthly payments. For example, having a car note or a mortgage can round out your credit reports and help you obtain a good score. Different credit scores get calculated in different ways, but if the amount you owe on your revolving debt is more than 30% of your available credit limit, it may have a negative impact on your scores.

On the other hand, having a bunch of inactive cards in your wallet isn't ideal either. High unused revolving credit limits can also hurt your score. Why? This is because we can easily get into a lot of debt really quickly with the credit we already have, and carrying high revolving balances increases the chances that we could have trouble paying back any additional credit that can have a huge negative impact. There is always an exception to the rule: when you have had the revolving lines open and without use for more than twenty-four months, this signals to the underwriter that you are well disciplined in your financial matters.

**Key Factors Affecting Your Score**

There are two key factors that can affect your credit score:

*1. Number of accounts with delinquency:* Missed and late payments—including the number of late payments, how late they were, and how recently they occurred—are important to FICO Scores.

*2. Too many inquiries in the last twelve months:* This will adversely affect your credit score. FICO scores look at the number of times a person applies for credit since we oftentimes actively seek credit, which tends to pose a risk to lenders than those who are not. Eight (8) is a great FICO score with Trans-Union. Other reporting agencies vary.

I have included below information for all three major credit bureaus.

- Call TransUnion at 844-456-0942, every Monday to Friday, from 8:00 a.m. to 9:00 p.m. EST (www.transunion.com)

- Call Equifax at 866-640-2273. They are open seven days a week, from 8:00 a.m. to 3:00 a.m. EST (www.equifax.com).

- Call Experian at 800-854-7201, every Monday to Friday from 7:00 a.m. to 8:00 p.m., Saturdays from 7:00 a.m. to 8:00 p.m., and Sundays from 7:00 a.m. to 7:00 p.m. EST (www.experian.com).

### Debt

Debt can cause all sorts of problems in our lives, both financially and spiritually. When we obtain too much debt, it is as if we become trapped, in a downward spiral, or drowning in our finances. Our worries over our debt quickly consume our lives and our thoughts. We become a servant to our debt. Our debt then becomes our master. Debt can cause us to lose sight of a carefree life. We begin to live our lives consumed by worries of financial burdens instead of putting God first in our lives. We can quickly forget about God and the ones we love and care for, being consumed or overwhelmed with debt and worry.

In our world today, many of us find ourselves in financial debt over our heads. We try to understand how we got to this point. We often incur debt by buying things that are far from necessary, and its effect. When the amount we incur is substantial, it diminishes our sense of worth, diminishes our hope for the future, and almost eliminates our sensitivity to the needs of others around us— such as family, friends, coworkers, and ministries.

**What Do Your Credit Scores Say to Lenders/Underwriters?**

The following chart gives a visual representation of what your credit scores say to lenders and underwriters.

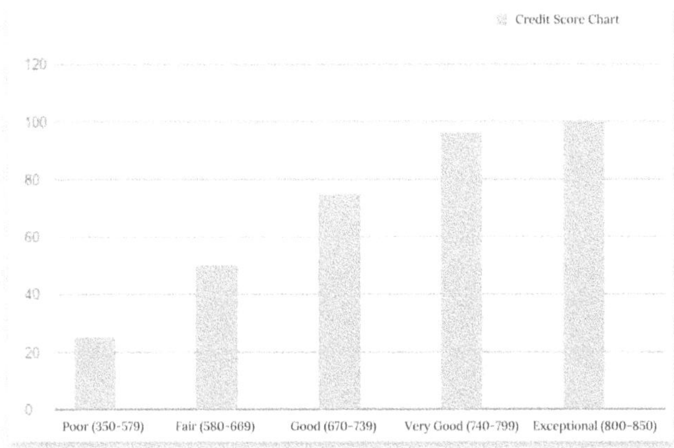


*Poor*: 350–579
*Fair*: 580–669
*Good*: 670–739
*Very Good:* 740–799
*Exceptional:* 800–850

Anything under *620* could make it harder to get a mortgage loan. Anything above *700* is more attractive to lenders.

From the underwriter's viewpoint, we are graded as:

- A paper - Exceptional scores (800 and above)
- B paper - Very Good scores (740–799)
- C paper - Good scores (670–739)
- D paper - Fair scores (580–669)
- F paper - Poor scores (350–579)

Now, let's put this in plain terms. An underwriter pulls a tri-merge credit report when applying for a mortgage of any type:

purchase, refinance, or home equity loan. Also, the report is pulled within ninety days of the loan application. A tri-merge report is from all three major credit bureaus. If you are planning to purchase, refinance, or apply for a home equity loan, you should not have any new inquiries 120 days prior to the application as this could potentially have your loan application denied for too many recent inquires. When the tri-merge report is pulled, the underwriter takes the middle score of the three reporting agencies. For example, if your scores are: TransUnion (675), Equifax (700), and Experian (715), then the score used for your mortgage loan would be 700.

Credit report red flags can cause your loan application to be denied or pending approval. To avoid receiving red flags, you want to review all credit reports prior to application to address possible red flags and Social Security number mismatches. Also, check all creditors for accuracy. Lastly, clear any and all public records (refer back to Chapter 6). Fix any errors and rerun credit, if necessary. Having a clean credit report is key to getting the loan approved. Also, having three months in reserve funds is important to getting to the closing table.

If you still have derogatory information listed on your credit report, you will need a derogatory credit letter of explanation (LOX). This letter is required when the automatic underwriting system gives the loan officer a reply of refer or caution. The borrower is to provide a signed and dated letter of explanation regarding derogatory credit listed in the credit report. Be sure to include details such as divorce, bankruptcy, hardship, loss of employment, seasonal work, etc.

To have child support or alimony included as debt or income, you must provide supporting documentation for at least three years. If less than three years, the underwriter will exclude this from debt or income ratios. Child support or alimony debt provides divorce decree, separation agreement, or child support order verifying monthly payment for any child support/alimony obligations (FYI, original documents from the judge, signed and stamped from the courthouse, are the only ones accepted).

Now, there will be times when you have made inquiries from

potential creditors prior to the threshold of 120 days. If this is the case, you will need to submit a credit inquiry letter of explanation (LOX). This is required if you have new credit inquiries within 120 days of loan application specifying if new debt has been opened (most lenders will exclude subject inquiries and noncredit utility inquires).

* * *

### *Prayer to Stay the Course*

*Father God, we come humbly before You to say thank You. Thank You, dear God, that You never sleep nor slumber. Thank You that You are our shield and buckler, protecting us from hurt, harm, or danger, seen or unseen. Thank You, God, for we adore You. We worship You! We magnify Your Most Holy Name! You are Alpha and Omega. The beginning and the end. You knew our beginning before we became living human beings. You have planned our future, and we thank You for Your patience with us. Thank You that You don't give up on us as some people do. Thank You that You never grow weary and Your Spirit is with us everywhere we go.*

*Holy Spirit, You are welcome to come in. Thank You, God, for a sound mind, a mind that is able to make strategic decisions, decisions that will catapult us into living a debt-free life. Help us to step out of our fears and walk in faith. Increase our faith. Help us to exercise our faith. Faith is action and movement.*

*Help us to budget and stick to the plan to pay off any existing debt. God, we believe that You can pay off our debt supernaturally, so we are putting our faith into action by starting to tackle the current debt we owe so that we may be prepared and ready for debt cancellation in this season.*

*Help us create our budgets and balance sheets that will give us a visual picture of our finances and spending habits so that we can and we will be free—totally free. No more baggage, no more heavyweights, no more stress over unsurmountable debt, and no more bondage. Free to walk in the liberty and unity of the promises of God of abundance and prosperity, wealth and riches, health and wholeness, and our Kingdom authority.*

*Father God, if we have sinned against thee or a brother or sister, we ask for forgiveness of our sins by omission or commission. Transform our hearts, Lord. Transform our minds. Transform our soul. For our desire is to please You, God. Our desire is to love as You have loved us. Our desire is to encourage ourselves and others in the Lord. Our desire is to see all that You have promised us come to existence in our lifetime.*

*We thank You for wisdom, knowledge, understanding, and the ability to create wealth, Kingdom wealth. Lord, keep our minds, ears, and eyes open to receive wise counsel regarding our financial matters. Help us to trust again. We thank You in advance that we will be good stewards of our financial resources. We will steward our credit reports with due diligence, pulling our reports annually, and reviewing anything that needs to be removed.*

*Father God, Your word tells us to seek You first the kingdom of God and Your righteousness, and all these things shall be added unto us. Take the wheel, God. We desire to receive all that You have in store for us, that You will be pleased with our work and commitment to open up the windows of heaven, and pour out blessings that we won't have room to contain.*

*In the matchless Name and Authority of Christ*
*Jesus, we pray. Amen.*

> Do not withhold good from those to whom it is due when it is in your power to act. Do not say to your neighbor, 'Come back tomorrow and I'll give it to you'—when you already have it with you.
>
> — PROVERBS 3:27-28 (NIV)

# 8

# IDENTITY THEFT

> Whoever loves money never has enough; whoever loves wealth is never satisfied with their income. This too is meaningless.
>
> — ECCLESIASTES 5:10 NIV

America is currently experiencing enormous reports of identity theft. With scammers and identity thieves operating across the globe, nations are experiencing problems. The advancement of technology has been revolutionizing the world. As a result, most consumers have shifted to buying and selling things online, which has added to the identity theft crisis. Many small business owners and entrepreneurs have not been able to recover. The "mom-and-pop" business is almost a thing of the past.

People who steal others' identities will use your credit score, bank accounts, social security number, and your assets. They use the things you have worked hard to achieve through self-control and self-discipline. As a result, they will live a life that is not true to them, but rather it is your truth.

As a result of worrying too much about what other people think rather than what God thinks, you adopt the identities of the people you read about, see on television, or follow on social media, rather than remaining true to yourself. Worrying about other people's acceptance of you is one of the greatest strongholds to overcome. What is the cause of this stronghold?

The Word of God helps us understand this more clearly. In Galatians 1, we read about the religious leaders called Judaizers who sought to place believers under a performance standard "under the law," thereby abandoning grace. In Galatians 1:10, Paul talks about these well-meaning, Bible-quoting leaders who were ripping the saints off and pulling them away from God's grace. Paul says, "Am I now seeking the faith of man or God? Or am I serving to please men? If I were still trying to please men, I would not be a bond-servant of Christ" (Galatians 1:10). Paul is saying that it is possible to be more people-orientated than God-orientated. In Proverbs 29:25 (NASB), it says, "The fear of man brings a snare, but he who trusts in the Lord will be exalted." Satan uses your legitimate need for acceptance in an illegitimate way, resulting in you living under a false identity.

Pay attention. You'll notice how confused people are when they try to please everyone. One minute they are pleasing one person, and the next minute, they are pleasing someone else. These people must be around others who make them feel good; otherwise, they become depressed. These people are called people-pleasers. How do you begin to overcome these strongholds of worrying about what others think? It is when you decide what God says about you that matters most.

Know what God has for you; His plan is designed, specifically and especially, for you. God doesn't give your blessings to others. He prepares you for the blessing that He has in store for you by taking you through the process. He matures you, as a Believer, so that you no longer need milk, but can eat meat instead. Despite your ugly tears, messed-up hair days, days without make-up, and rants, God still loves you! If you allow yourself to be driven by people's approval, just remember, people are fallible, and their emotions shift. Your identity determines your destiny. So, you must protect your identity, both naturally and spiritually– which brings me to our next point of reference. Do you know what to do if you are a victim of identity theft?

**Five Steps to Take When You Are a Victim of Identity Theft**

1) *File an initial fraud alert/ file with one agency.* The agency you select will report that information to the other two agencies. It's normally free to file. The three major credit reporting agencies you can use are Experian, Equifax, and TransUnion.

2) *Initiate a credit freeze.* This denies anyone from looking up your credit. If you want to know how long the freeze can stay on your credit report, contact your state's attorney general's office. This is generally free to victims of identity theft. If there is a fee, it's normally a small fee, like $10. Place alerts on the three credit reporting agencies, previously mentioned, and request a copy of your credit report when filing the fraud alert. This is free to victims of fraud and identity theft. Look over each report in detail to see what is not yours.

3. *File an identity theft report with local authorities and the federal agency.* The report helps you get fraudulent information removed from your credit report, which stops businesses and collection agencies from coming after you for debts that are not yours.

> Filing a report is a two-part process. The *Federal Trade Commission* is a government agency that helps protect you, the consumer, from fraud. You can file this report online at https://reportfraud.ftc.gov/#/ and complete your report. After completing your report, you will be issued an FTC Identity Theft Affidavit. Print this report, and keep it for your records.
>
> Then, you will need to file a police report in person, or you may be able to do this online. Check with your local police

department for instructions and the items you will need to file the report for proof of your identity. After filing a police report, ask for a copy of the report and the filing number.

After completing the FTC Affidavit and obtaining a police report filing number, you have a complete identity theft report. Now, you are ready to take on each fraudulent item that you may have discovered in your credit report.

4. *Contact credit bureaus, lenders, and businesses, and file a dispute with the fraud department of each company and each credit reporting agency.* While this may be time-consuming, it's important for you to take good notes and keep all records. Make note of their names, the date, and the time you spoke with them, and write down any instructions given by the fraud department. The FTC has many helpful resources, and they provide a checklist for how to dispute different claims.

(If you desire assistance, contact us via website: www.trifold-connectionsllc.com, email: info@trifoldconnectionsllc.com, or phone 708-553-0002)

5. *Place an extended fraud alert on file with each reporting credit agency.* This alert is free and lasts for seven years. It allows you to receive two free credit reports a year to stay on top of any new or suspicious activity. Also, during this time of the health crisis, the FTC website allows monthly reports for no additional charge. There are more than the three major credit reporting agencies; so, check your local listings for other reporting agencies and contact them, as well.

## You Gamble on Life, So Gamble on God

In these times, God's people must trust Him to rest their bodies, minds, and souls. When you choose to trust God (rather than trying to please God), you enter into the realm of faith, believing in what cannot be seen; yet, acting as if you can see it. It's a gamble!

> Now, faith is confidence in what we hope for and assurance about what we do not see.
>
> — HEBREWS 11:1 NIV

Your identity and positioning in Christ are unseen in the physical world. In fact, the world screams out the opposite, telling you that you are a failure, guilty, and inadequate. It takes real faith to act on God's proclamation that you are accepted, forgiven, and complete in Christ. Yes, faith is putting your trust in Him, and what He says is true. Faith is putting your lives in His hands, even though you can't see or trace Him.

> By faith, we understand that the universe was formed at God's command, so that what is seen was not made out of what was visible.
>
> — HEBREWS 11:3 NIV

The physical evidence for God's creation is conclusive; yet, it still takes faith for you and me to believe that God created the universe because we weren't there to see it happen. I also believe it takes faith to believe that God has made you new creatures in Christ! Anyone who comes to Christ must believe that He exists and that He rewards those who earnestly seek Him (Hebrews 11:6).

Blaise Pascal, the famous French philosopher, physicist, and mathematician put it this way, "Belief is a wise wager. Granted that faith cannot be proved, what harm will come to you if you gamble on its truth, and it proves false? If you gain, you gain all; if you lose, you lose nothing. Wager, then, without hesitation, that He exists."

### The God Who Cares

God hears you when you pray. It's that simple and that profound. Unless you sit in this truth, you will miss how incredible and life-altering this is.

In 1 Peter 5, the disciple Peter tells us to humble ourselves before the Lord and to cast our cares upon Him. He explains that we have an adversary who is attacking us and that Believers throughout the world are suffering. In the seventh verse, he tells us to cast our cares upon the Lord, because He cares for us.

How often do we take this for granted? Of course, He cares for us, but think about it for a moment. Why should He? Don't forget, the same Bible that makes this statement also tells us that all human beings have rejected God (Romans 1), that everyone has sinned and refuses to seek after God (Romans 3), and that we are all dead in our sins (Ephesians 2). There is no logical step between "we have all rejected him" and "He cares for us all." And yet, there it is– illogical but real.

Consider this statement, "God cares for you." So, cast your cares upon Him, and lay every burden down at His feet. He cares about you and wants to hear what's concerning you. It's that simple, but this simple realization will change your life. Let it! Right this second, God is listening to you and me. Because He cares, He hears. He's listening and waiting to hear your voice, so say something to Him. Practice believing that He is listening and cares what we will say. Then, say something– anything– because He hears.

**How to Pray for Your True Identity**

Before we pray concerning our true identity, let's examine the Word of God in Matthew.

*The World Is Not A Stage*

> "Be especially careful when you are trying to be good so that you don't make a performance out of it. It might be good theater, but the God who made you won't be applauding.
>
> When you do something for someone else, don't call attention to yourself. You've seen them in action, I'm

> sure—"playactors" I call them—treating prayer meeting and street corner alike as a stage, acting compassionate as long as someone is watching, playing to the crowds. They get applause, true, but that's all they get. When you help someone out, don't think about how it looks. Just do it—quietly and unobtrusively. That is the way your God, who conceived you in love, working behind the scenes, helps you out.
>
> — MATTHEW 6:1-4 MSG

*Pray With Simplicity*

And when you come before God, don't turn that into a theatrical production either. All these people making a regular show out of their prayers, hoping for fifteen minutes of fame! Do you think God sits in a box seat?

Here's what I want you to do: Find a quiet, secluded place so you won't be tempted to role-play before God. Just be there as simply and honestly as you can manage. The focus will shift from you to God, and you will begin to sense his grace.

The world is full of so-called prayer warriors who are prayer-ignorant. They're full of formulas and programs and advice, peddling techniques for getting what you want from God. Don't fall for that nonsense. This is your Father you are dealing with, and he knows better than you what you need. With a God like this loving you, you can pray very simply. Like this:

*Our Father in heaven,*
*Reveal who you are.*
*Set the world right;*
*Do what's best—*
*as above, so below.*
*Keep us alive with three square meals.*
*Keep us forgiven with you and forgiving others.*
*Keep us safe from ourselves and the Devil.*

*You're in charge!*
*You can do anything you want!*
*You're ablaze with beauty!*
*Yes. Yes. Yes.*

— Matthew 6:9-13 MSG

In prayer, there is a connection between what God does and what you do. You can't get forgiveness from God, for instance, without also forgiving others. If you refuse to do your part, you cut yourself off from God's part.

> When you practice some appetite-denying discipline to better concentrate on God, don't make a production out of it. It might turn you into a small-time celebrity but it won't make you a saint. If you "go into training" inwardly, act normal outwardly. Shampoo and comb your hair, brush your teeth, and wash your face. God doesn't require attention-getting devices. He won't overlook what you are doing; he'll reward you well.
>
> — MATTHEW 6:16-18 MSG

* * *

***Prayer for Your True Identity***

*Dear God, I believe that You exist. I believe that by trusting You, I am pleasing You. Today, by the promise of Your Holy Spirit, my counselor, I choose to believe what You say is true about me. I am loved, adopted, accepted, chosen, appointed, anointed, and cherished by You in and through Christ Jesus!*

*Father God, protect our identities from falling victim to the world's systems/technology. With new technology developing daily, Father, help us to protect our identities and the identity of our family members and loved ones.*

*Help us, Father, to embrace our true identities in Christ Jesus. Help us not to be ashamed of who we are. Help us stand boldly in our faith, proclaiming Your good news and promises of 'yes' and 'amen' in our lives! Increase our wisdom, knowledge, and understanding; increase our ability to exercise self-discipline and self-control.*

*Keep us FOCUSed (Following One Course Until Successful). Continue to cut away the things and obstacles in our lives that keep us from growing and maturing in our kingdom walk and assignments.*

*I break off any chains of bondage keeping us in a poverty mindset. I decree and declare financial wealth, and a sound mind to make difficult decisions concerning investing in ourselves and into the kingdom of God.*

*I decree and declare that we will become fiscally fit and use our time, talents, and treasures in building up God's kingdom here on earth. I release an overflow of creativity in the hearts and minds of God's people. I release a servant's heart. You said in Your Word that if we want to be first, we must become the last or the least of them, serving one another in spirit and in truth, loving one another to wholeness.*

*God, allow humility, integrity, character, overflow, and abundance to be our portion. God, we have taken a gamble on many things in this world. Now, allow us to take a gamble on You. For You said in Your Word that we are winners, overcomers, conquerors, and victors.*

*We trust You even when we can't trace you; help us to love our enemies as we love ourselves. We thank You, God, that You care for us and desire to see us prosper spiritually, physically, emotionally, and financially. You help us to be good stewards of the many blessings You have already bestowed upon us and the many blessings still to come.*

*God, You want us to know that You hear our prayers and that You listen to every word that comes out of our mouths, even the unspoken words of our hearts. You transform our hearts and heal us in our broken areas. You desire to have an intimate relationship with us. So, we put all of our hearts' concerns on the altar before You to work it out! We know that You love and care for us, no matter our status, addictions, unhealthy habits, unworthiness, or brokenness. God, You always meet us right where we are.*

*Your Word says, "My grace is sufficient for you, for my power is made perfect in weakness" (2 Corinthians 12:9 KJV). Everyone who is born of flesh and blood is weak, but not everyone is aware of their weaknesses because they are not God-fearing. Help us, God, to humble ourselves before You and proclaim to a dying world that You are Lord!*

*I ask, God, that You cover these prayers in Your Son Jesus' Blood of the New Covenant, letting our requests be known unto You, God, who is the author and finisher of our faith.*

*In Jesus' mighty Authority, we pray. Amen.*

* * *

> “Anyone who has been stealing must steal no longer, but must work, doing something useful with their own hands, that they may have something to share with those in need.
>
> — EPHESIANS 4:28 (NIV)

# 9

# PREPARATION FOR FINAL LOAN APPROVAL DOCUMENTATION

> 'For I know the plans I have for you' says the LORD. 'They are plans for good and not for disaster, to give you a future and a hope.'
>
> —JEREMIAH 29:11 NLT

We have made some great progress in learning the skills needed to be wise stewards over our finances and learning about due diligence in the matters of our credit reporting. Now, we have come to what potential items you will need for final loan approval of your mortgage for purchases, refinance, home equity loans, and other installment loans. The ultimate goal is to get to the closing table and build a complete financial portfolio.

I will now share with you the terms and their meanings, why it's important to have these documents, and what needs to be included in your Letters of Explanation (LOX) prepared for the underwriter:

## Credit

There are nine critical terms associated with *credit* for us to review:

- *Mortgage Note:* In the United States of America, a mortgage note is a promissory note secured by a specified mortgage loan. Mortgage notes are a written promise to repay a specified sum of money plus interest at a specified rate and length of time to fulfill the promise. This is for an existing mortgage to corroborate (confirm) benefits to the borrower if not evident per transaction. It includes terms such as the total amount of the home loan, the down payment amount, and whether monthly or bimonthly payments are required.

- *Verification of Rent/Mortgage (VOR or VOM):* Verification of rent/mortgage is a letter requested by the mortgage lender wanting to verify your housing payments for the previous twelve to twenty-four months. If the mortgage is not reporting on the credit report or VOR is needed to satisfy the requirement for underwriting final loan approval, do yourself a favor and have this information completed at the time of application. In the case of a home purchase, more is better.

- *Derogatory Credit:* A letter of explanation for past derogatory credit is a must when applying for your home loan. If there is an item on your account that is past due or at risk, which is the risk that a lender may lose the money they've lent you due to missed required payments. In this LOX, be specific on why this information is reflected on your credit report: divorce, getting laid off, loss of job, seasonal employment, etc. Preparation is key. Take your time in preparing this detailed information. The underwriter doesn't know you personally, so the more detailed information provided, the more the underwriter can make a decision in your favor.

- *Current Home Under Contract:* This is one for when a seller has accepted a buyer's offer to purchase the property. But before the sale of the home can actually close, certain contingencies (home appraisal, home inspection, buyer financing, etc.) must first be met; otherwise, the deal can still fall through. You may be able to exclude current PITI (principal-interest-taxes-insurance) in your debt-to-income ratios with a fully executed sales agreement for the borrower's current property not yet sold and closed and not selling prior to closing. A good nugget is to keep your loan officer informed of the details of your transaction. Communication is paramount.

- *New Debt:* Documentation verifying the terms of any new debt recently opened and not yet shown on your credit report. The best rule of thumb prior to making a big-ticket-item purchase is not to make any new credit accounts or have your credit run six months prior to the application or 1003 URLA (Uniform Residential Loan Application). This could make or break your ability to purchase that ideal home. Prior to purchasing your home, it may be a good idea not to have any recent inquiries on your credit report for a twelve-month period. It shows the underwriter your self-discipline and accountability to your existing budget and indebtedness.

- *Disputed Trade Lines:* When you decide to dispute trade lines on your current credit report, be sure to have pen and paper ready to record all details communicated between you and the creditor. Record things like the date, time, person you spoke to and their title, details of the agreed resolution (settlement), and a written agreement from the creditor (via fax, email, or postal mail) stating the resolution of the dispute. This is your proof to the underwriter that an agreement has been made to resolve any and all disputed trade lines. Documentation of resolution or explanation for disputed trade lines is needed to get to the final loan approval stage and to the closing table.

- *Payoff:* If you are required to pay off debts to qualify for the loan, be sure to include all creditors' letters with payoff information in the application with your loan officer. If funds are from an existing mortgage being sold, a release of mortgage or mortgage satisfaction letter will be required, stating funds received at closing, with documentation (a recent bank statement or proof of funds available on deposit in your financial institution).

- *Credit Card (CC) Statements:* If proceeds from your refinance or home equity loan are for debt consolidation, then you must provide the most recent CC statements for credit card balances being paid with loan funds at closing. This documentation is a must. Your underwriter will request a recent CC statement or a payoff letter from your creditor prior to closing. If this letter is not presented within the allotted time, your loan could be denied based on debt-to-income ratios.

- *Deferred Student Loan:* You will need to present the underwriter with a verified deferment letter for twelve or more months to exclude debt from ratios for portfolio/non-agency. This is necessary because when qualifying for your purchase if debt/income ratios exceed the lender's guidelines, this information will help in your qualifications to meet the lender guidelines. As discussed earlier, debt-to-income ratios ideally are 28/40 (28% in income and 40% for debt).

## Income

There are nine essential terms associated with *income* for us to review:

- *Profit and Loss (P&L) Statement:* This statement is needed if you have your own business. If you are using income from your business to qualify for the loan, you must have your profit and loss statements available for review. Audited YTD (year-to-date) P&L/financials are required if attempting to use current year self-employed income to qualify.

- *Lease Agreements:* Lease agreements are needed for those who have investment properties. You will be required to document rental income from rental properties being used to qualify. A complete lease agreement states the length of the lease, any up-front fees, the full address of the unit(s) being rented, monthly rent payment(s), and the rules and regulations governing the property's use.

- *Dividend/Interest:* Corresponding assets statements verifying the existence of sufficient remaining assets to justify the use of dividend, interest, or capital gain income. Common examples of dividend/interest or capital gain income are interest earned on savings account(s) and dividend earnings from stock and mutual funds. Capital gain income is an increase in capital asset value and is realized when the asset is sold. Capital gains apply to any type of asset, including investments and those purchased for personal use. This may be short-term (one year or less) or long-term (more than one year), and this income must be claimed on your income taxes.

- *Employment Contract:* Many Americans are now independent contractors and freelancers; as an independent contractor, you will need to document your current contract and any future employment or contract terms.

- *Child Support/Alimony:* To qualify to use income from child support or alimony, you must present documentation that reflects six months' bank statements or canceled checks for any child support or alimony income used in qualifying for your purchase.

- *K-1s (Business Owners):* All per schedule E on tax returns. Review 1040 schedule E for partnerships and S corps to determine the need for K-1s. Provide all business returns if ownership exceeds 25% per K-1s.

- *1099 Forms:* These may be requested to document the source of consulting-type income run through business returns or Schedule C.

- *Bonus/Overtime:* A letter from your employer documenting the continuance of bonus and/or OT income may be requested. If it is requested, you must present this letter on company letterhead, with detailed information of the length of time the bonus/overtime will continue, complete with contact information of the employer or human resource department.

- *Capital Gains:* As stated above, this should appear on your most recent two years' 1040 tax returns, plus any/all corresponding assets to support three years' continuance.

**Property**

There are ten essential terms associated with *properties* for us to review:

- *Condo Documentation.* There is more documentation needed for a condo purchase. A condo is governed by its bylaws, questionnaire, and homeowner 6 insurance policy. All of these documents are required before receiving a final loan approval.

- *Survey:* In most states in the United States, there is no survey required. I recommend putting this in your budget to have your own survey completed for your records. Note: In some cases, a survey will be completed by the lender. An existing property survey is needed for New York and Florida properties.

- *Inspections:* A final home inspection is necessary. You want to know if your new home has pests or other insect infestations. If your lender doesn't require an inspection, I encourage you to have a final inspection completed for your best interest. It's best to conduct pest or other inspections as disclosed in the purchase agreement.

- *Personal Property:* If you decide to include personal property as part of the sale, you should list its value or worth. If the seller conveys, "I will leave this furniture as a gift to you upon purchasing the property," be sure it is shown on your *purchase contract.* This is called valuation documentation for personal property being included in a sale contract.

- *Title Setup Form:* This is to be submitted for settlement agents, not on the reviewed list. This is provided by the settlement agent, but I have included this information because you also want to review the title. There are three components that apply to the concept of a title: ownership, occupation or possession, and the right of possession. Note: In most states, an attorney will review and approve the title.

- *Personal Property Being Removed (Investment Property):* According to United States law, property that is left behind by a tenant is typically assumed to be abandoned after a specific time frame. This time frame can be anywhere between one week and one year. If the property remains unclaimed during this time frame, it may be disposed of or sold in order to recoup storage costs. In a fully executed purchase contract addendum, removing personal property from said property should be included in the purchase contract.

- *Hazard Insurance:* It is the buyer's responsibility to secure homeowners insurance once you have a final loan approval. The declaration page for the subject property (HO6 for condo) is required.

- *Homeowner's Insurance*: This is a form of property insurance that covers losses and damages to an individual's house and assets in the home. The policy usually covers interior damage, exterior damage, loss or damage of personal assets, and injury that arises while on your property. Every homeowners' insurance policy has a liability limit that determines the amount of coverage the insured has should an unfortunate incident occur. Homeowner's insurance should not be confused with a home warranty or with mortgage insurance.

- *For Condominium Homeowners Insurance, an HO6 Is Required:* This covers your unit. Now outside your unit, you have rights and/or an interest in the common areas of the property, but the condo or co-op association may have primary responsibility for insuring that portion of the property. HO6 protects your unit and everything it contains; it provides liability coverage, loss of use coverage, and more. For more information, contact your insurance provider. Lastly, whenever a claim is made on any of the above-listed incidents, the homeowner will be required to pay a deductible ($250, $500, or $1,000 deductible— the higher the deductible, the lower your premium for homeowners insurance), which, in effect, is the out-of-pocket costs for the insured.

- *Principal Interest Tax Insurance (PITI):* The underwriter will request documentation to verify property, taxes, homeowner insurance (HOI), and homeowner association (HOA) amounts for other real estate owned. Note: If your down payment is less than 20%, you will be required to carry PITI.

- *Extension/Addendum to Contract:* There will be situations where you might need an extension/addendum to your purchase contract. The extension should be requested to cover the estimated close date.

### Miscellaneous FHA/VA

There are five miscellaneous *FHA/VA* terms for us to review:

- *Veteran Affairs:* Veteran Affairs (VA) Certificate of Eligibility, VA Form DD 214 (Certificate of Release or Discharge from Active Duty), VA verification of VA Benefits Form, VA Nearest Relative Form, VA Case Number Verification Form, VA counseling checklist for military homebuyer(s), VA indebtedness questionnaire, amendatory agreement for purchases, addendum to application form purchases.

- *VA Condo:* If a VA owns a condo, please confirm condo is VA eligible by accessing the VA Loan Guaranty site at: https://vip.vba.va.gov/portal/VBAH/VBAHome/condopudsearch.

- *Social Security Card:* The underwriter will require your government-issued Social Security card as evidence of your Social Security number on FHA loans and FHA streamline loans.

- *Mortgage Statements:* Current mortgage statements to document current mortgage insurance payment (MIP) amount on FHA loans and FHA streamline loans. MIP can be avoided with a 20% down payment or more.

- *Telephone FHA Applications:* The following documents need to be signed or dated by the mortgage loan officer (MLO). It must be signed on the day of application, and the Important Notice to Homeowners signed on the same day as the application, and the Informed Consumer Choice Disclosure signed and dated on the day of the application. FHA refinance authorization is good through the month of funding the loan.

* * *

### Prayer of New Opportunities & Opened Doors

*First, God, we thank You for being God Almighty— the All-Sufficient One, All-Powerful One, and God of another chance.*

*We thank You, God, that You forgive us of our sins, and You throw them into the sea of forgetfulness.*
*We humbly ask that You break down the walls we may have built up against You, God, or our fellow man.*
*God, give us the heart to want to forgive others and ourselves for things*

*we have done in secret or openly for forgiveness is not natural but spiritual.*

*God, we thank You for a sound mind, a mind that will chase after Your righteousness, which is simply to live right before You and the world that we live in.*
*God, create in us a clean heart and renew a right spirit within us.*

*God, we desire to live as Your Word has promised us, living a debt-free life, owing no man a debt, but to love one another as Your Word has commanded us. Help us to love our neighbors as ourselves.*

*We thank You for the ability to gain wisdom, knowledge, and understanding. Help us, Abba Father, to apply the principles and precepts being taught so that I and my family may live in the overflow, abundance, and prosperity that You have for us through obedience.*
*We thank You for life, health, strength, and the ability to make strategic decisions.*

*We thank You that You will help us to do away with debt. We believe in Your supernatural abilities of debt cancellation.*

*We will be good stewards of our financial matters and our credit-reporting history. God, we ask that You keep us FOCUSed:*

**F**ollowing
**O**ne
**C**oursc
**U**ntil
**S**uccessful

*Help us to be steadfast and unmovable in creating our budgets and sticking to them. Help us to begin a debt repayment plan, and instead of our money ruling us, You give us the ability to rule over our money.*

*We thank You that You are the rewarder of all good deeds. We know that by being obedient to Your Word, You will do miraculous things in our lives.*

*Help us to be humble and kind, judging no one, for Your Word tells us not to judge for the same measure we judge others that You would judge us.*

*Thank You for a heart of forgiveness, love, kindness, joy, and peace that surpasses all understanding, goodness, faithfulness, and being able to forbear one another in love.*

*God, as we begin to tackle our indebtedness, give us the mindset to stay consistent, dedicated, and committed until we have achieved the "art of budgeting." Help us to invest in ourselves and our family inheritance.*

*Lastly, Holy Spirit, open our eyes to see, open our ears to hear, and open our hearts to feel what the Spirit of the Lord is saying in this time and in this season. I will always give You the praise, worship, and honor in all things.*

*In Jesus' Name and Authority, we humbly pray. Amen.*

> “It is better not to make a vow than to make one and not fulfill it.
>
> — ECCLESIASTES 5:5 (NIV)

MONEY
LIFE
FAMILY
JOURNEY

# 10

# IS THERE A SECRET TO SUCCESS?

## (VOLUME 3 BONUS CHAPTER)

> Beloved, I wish above all things that thou mayest prosper and be in health, even as thy soul prospereth.
>
> — 3 JOHN 1:2 KJV

Before we get started in this bonus chapter, I would like to share a personal testimony with you. At the end of 2019, I put out on Facebook that I had gotten married. You should have seen the responses that I received. It was overwhelming, to say the least.

I want to share with you the revelation that God gave me on December 4, 2019. He said, "Daughter, when you put up things from your personal life, the people jump all over that, wanting more to be revealed. People are concerned more about what is going on with you personally than learning the tools necessary to live this life in abundance, wealth, overflow, prosperity, and healthy living. When I have you come up every week pouring out biblical principles and precepts on wisdom, knowledge, and understanding of what my

Word says about finances, debt, investments, inheritance, and how to apply my word, my precepts, to acquire these things, there's a different audience and very little responses. Do not get discouraged, stay on the wall, and continue to be steadfast and unmovable, always abounding in the work of the Kingdom. For in due season, all of your sowing into the lives of My people, I shall repay."

So to settle everyone's inquiring minds, I married God on December 4, 2019. I have surrendered my life, my heart, my will, my emotions, my children, my family, and my very being over to God. With God at the head of my life, I know everything is going to be all right. I'm not saying that trouble, trials, and tribulations won't come knocking at my door. I am saying, "I surrender them all to my Father, who never leaves me nor forsakes me." He loves us unconditionally, and He supplies all of our needs. He provides more than enough. I am living in the overflow of God's promises.

God desires to bless all His children. The blessings of financial security, wealth, health, and His wisdom, it's yours. It's yours for the asking. It's yours for the taking. How bad do you want it? Anything worth having is worth sacrificing for. Remember this: "You are a divine original fashioned by God to be radiantly beautiful."

We must make sacrifices to reach our goals and become successful. We must get committed and stay consistent. We must learn to say no and mean no and not allow others to manipulate us into the ways of the world or keep us stuck in systems that are not working for us. We must be able to walk away, even when those people are trying to control our decisions, trying to keep us in a place of low self-esteem. It's time to stand up and get aggressive about our future.

So, let's begin with insight into the upcoming Volume III, "Is There a Secret to Success?" and let's receive the Word of the Lord regarding our financial matters. For we know and some of us are learning that God's Word has much to say about money, savings, investments, and inheritance.

## What Is True Success?

True success comes from obedience and doing the will of Our Father, God. True success is in fulfilling the original purpose for which we have been created. Everything else is suspect.

Successful people are driven by a divine unique purpose. Successful people are overcomers and innovators. We conquer kingdoms, create nations, and reshape and shape history. History does not make us; rather, we make history. When we dare to come out of our comfort zone, think with an entirely different mindset (right-brain dominance—creative, intuitive, arts, creation, feeling, and imagination), obey the will of God, and follow His divine purpose, then we will leave our own legacy in this world for generations to come.

If you want to influence the very world we live in, your life, and that of your family, your city, your community, and even the nation, you and I must realize that we are created with a divine, unique purpose—to be the change we want to see in our nation and the nations that make up the seven continents of this world.

## What Is Purpose?

In the Old Testament, the verbal root of the Hebrew word for *purpose* means "to give counsel, deliberate, purpose, or determine." In five passages where the noun appears, four refer to God's purpose, and one to the purpose of a person's heart (Proverbs 19:21, 20:5; Isaiah 46:10–11; and Jeremiah 32:19). I will share Isaiah with you:

> Remember the things I have done in the past. For I alone am God! I am God, and there is none like me. Only I can tell you the future before it even happens. Everything I plan will come to pass, for I do whatever I wish. I will call a swift bird of prey from the east—a leader from a distant land to come and do my bidding. I have said what I would do, and I will do it. 'Listen to

> me, you stubborn people who are so far from doing right. For I am ready to set things right, not in the distant future, but right now! I am ready to save Jerusalem and show my glory to Israel.'
>
> — ISAIAH 46:9–13 NLT

God desires to see us successful, wealthy, and prosperous. Wealth has been designed by God for the righteous. We see many in our land today who have wealth and use it wickedly and selfishly. As the above scripture reminds us, we must come into obedience to God and not man. We must take time to reflect on the goodness of God and all He has provided for us, our children, and our households, taking the time to meditate on our past mistakes and successes. There are lessons to be learned so that we will not repeat them again.

I promise you, I had a real issue with pleasing people. I wanted to be accepted and not rejected. I wanted to be in the crowd. I wanted to be liked. The more I wanted these desires, the more God allowed hurt, betrayal, deceit, and rejection to show their ugly heads. I had to retreat into reflection and meditation and ask God why so much pain. His response was "I am your God. You will have no other gods before me! I am your provider. It is I who supplies all your needs. It is I who loves you unconditionally. Cling to me, and I will show you all things and give you the desires of your heart."

In the introduction, I shared my story of my marriage to God. This is how I realized that people have good intentions, but they don't always follow their hearts. Also, some people, although they love you, may envy you or be jealous of your success. They will express in your presence, "I'm so proud of you" or "I will support you," and they never meant a word. How will you know this? You'll know this by their actions, not by the words they speak.

God is ready to set things right in the life of every believer, not in the distant future, but right now! You and I must pivot, obey, repent, and receive our full inheritance so that we too may leave a legacy in the earth for our children and the future generations to come after us.

### Defining Your Purpose

Here are some steps that can assist you in defining your purpose:

- Step 1: *Look for passion.* What is something you absolutely love and would do for free?

- Step 2: *Look for people.* Who are you serving?

- Step 3: *Look for impact.* What impact do you have on the people in your circle or community? How do the people you serve benefit from the work you do?

- Step 4: *Why do you exist?* Now, bring these ingredients together into a simple purpose statement.

*I exist to become the blessing to the body of Christ Jesus in order to advance the Kingdom of God here on earth as it is in Heaven! I exist to aid and assist my brothers and sisters to walk into your wealthy place in Christ Jesus, to know your true identities in Christ, and to encourage, enlighten, and empower the people of God in the commonwealth of the Kingdom, and to know just how powerful your words are, that you can speak a thing, and it shall come to pass!*

Now, I created a longer statement with details of my purpose. You would want to start off your purpose statement with one sentence and add it to your purpose statement as it becomes clearer and more defined to you.

*I exist to* _______________, *in order to* ____________________.

You want to be authentic in creating your purpose statement. It can be a challenge, but spend some time reflecting, and remember to journal your thoughts.

Clarifying what the Bible says about your purpose helps you in three important ways:

1. It declares why you exist.
2. It captures the heart of why you are on this earth and why Jesus died for you.
3. It defines your life—not in terms of what you think, but according to what God thinks. It anchors your life in the character and call of God.

### What Is Our Purpose According to God?

Our purpose on earth is to love God, and then show the same love He offers us to others so they can come to know Him. God wants us to lead others to Him through our love for them!

God's divine purpose for us is to have the mind of God toward others; it is God's intention about someone. God has a purpose for everyone and everything He created. Purpose is defined as the original intent of God for mankind. As human beings, we must come to the truth that we are a spirit with a dirt suit (the body), and we come from heaven, not earth. Please read all of Psalm 139 for a deeper understanding.

I want to further your knowledge by sharing that contrary to our belief of what we have been taught, life begins in heaven and not on earth. Since everything started in the mind of God, we were fully formed as God's idea in His mind before we received our physical bodies. Therefore, I have confidence in sharing this wisdom because we already existed and were given a divine authentic purpose by our Creator Elohim.

> “Before I formed you in the womb I knew you, and before you were born I consecrated you; I appointed you a prophet to the nations.

—JEREMIAH 1: 5 ESV

God is a god of purpose and intention. The scripture is loaded with purpose and God's intentionality.

**When Did God Call Us to Purpose?**

> [It is that purpose and grace] which He now has made known *and* has fully disclosed *and* made real [to us] through the appearing of our Savior Christ Jesus, Who annulled death *and* made it of no effect and brought life and immortality (immunity from eternal death) to light through the Gospel.
>
> — 2 TIMOTHY 1:10 AMPC

People who lack purpose often find themselves with low self-esteem and have a difficult time loving themselves for who they are, flaws and all, so most of them will begin to compete with others to prove themselves. They will imitate another's appearance, seek to assume that person's character or characteristics, seek to take the place of that individual or group, or attempt to steal the blessing that has been poured out on others. This competitive spirit arrives from a lack of knowing or a sense of your true identity and the absence of the truth, that each individual was born to be "a divine original fashioned by God to be radiantly beautiful" in life, on purpose! When you have not taken the time to reflect and determine your purpose, there is a great possibility you will feel insecure, inadequate, and insignificant.

> We will continue growing in faith, hope, and love. "These things will last forever—faith, hope, and love —and the greatest of these is love.
>
> — 1 CORINTHIANS 13:13 NLT

### Purpose Provides Significance

Purpose drives our lives to significance. *Significance*, according to dictionary.com, is "to have importance; of consequences." Once we find what drives our motivation, level of commitment, and consistency, we begin to make a difference in our own lives and the lives of our children and households, as well as the world we live in. Those who refuse to find their purpose or value live irresponsible lives and lifestyles. This is the reason we find individuals who are unhappy with everything, dissatisfied, angry, empty, depressed, unfocused, empty, and alone.

God has given us (human beings) a period of time to fulfill and complete our purpose here on earth. That is why it is essential for us to understand and start living a purpose-driven life and lifestyle as soon as possible. Take the opportunity to reflect, do self-care, meditate, and hear the still, small voice (the Holy Spirit) lead, guide, and direct you into purpose. We have no more time to waste on insignificant things that do *not* add value to our lives and the lives of others. You and I and every believer must embrace a clear and defined vision for our lives. It is time to pursue divine purpose and achieve the goals set before you.

I am sharing with you this passage of scripture to meditate and reflect on:

> "For everything there is a season, a time for every activity under heaven.
>
> A time to be born and a time to die. A time to plant and a time to harvest.
>
> A time to kill and a time to heal. A time to tear down and a time to build up.
>
> A time to cry and a time to laugh. A time to grieve and a time to dance.
>
> A time to scatter stones and a time to gather stones. A time to embrace and a time to turn away.

> A time to search and a time to quit searching. A time to keep and a time to throw away.
>
> A time to tear and a time to mend. A time to be quiet and a time to speak.
>
> A time to love and a time to hate. A time for war and a time for peace.
>
> What do people really get for all their hard work?
>
> I have seen the burden God has placed on us all.
>
> Yet God has made everything beautiful for its own time. He has planted eternity in the human heart, but even so, people cannot see the whole scope of God's work from beginning to end.
>
> So I concluded there is nothing better than to be happy and enjoy ourselves as long as we can.
>
> And people should eat and drink and enjoy the fruits of their labor, for these are gifts from God.
>
> And I know that whatever God does is final. Nothing can be added to it or taken from it. God's purpose is that people should fear him.
>
> What is happening now has happened before, and what will happen in the future has happened before, because God makes the same things happen over and over again.
>
> — ECCLESIASTES 3:1–15 NLT

As I close out this bonus chapter, consider these stats. There are statistics that tell us that savings and investments are at an all-time low. People are racking up credit card debt, revolving credit, buy now and pay later, and installment loans. If we continue in this world system, we will be flat broke and have absolutely nothing to show for all our hard work and time spent working for a secure life for our immediate family.

One of the things we can do as consumers is to have an accountability partner. An accountability partner is a person who will keep us motivated to stay on target for the goals and budgets we have set out to accomplish. Solomon challenged his readers to build accountability into their lives. Oftentimes than not, we crash when we try to do it alone.

An accountability partner is a person who coaches another person in terms of helping the other person keep their commitment. Not having an accountability partner to help you accomplish your goals is one of the main reasons 92% of people do not accomplish their goals and resolutions, according to a University of Scranton study by Dan Diamond in *Forbes* and an article by Dale Tyson.

My goal in life is to see you prosper and to help you reach your life goals, dreams, vision, and wealth in your finances. I am a financial consultant/adviser who would love to share my thirty-plus years of experience with you. If you are willing to follow and take heed of my advice, it can prevent a landslide of your future unfolding to less than what you imagined for your retirement and family inheritance. I can help you manage and create a financial plan that will bring you the success that you desire. Please keep in mind that *I am not* an accountability partner trying to run your life, but instead, I am a partner dedicated to helping you accomplish your goals, dreams, and financial stability. At the same time, I help you build your credit and FICO scores to be able to acquire debt that brings you assets with little or no cost to finance you. I will help you build a complete financial portfolio that will reflect and exemplify your beliefs, skills, qualifications, education, training, and experience.

Remember, you are not failures. If at first you don't succeed, try and try again.

Accountability is biblical, and it works! God is no respecter of persons! What He does for one, He can do for you and your household.

On most budget forms, the first line item is giving because we want to honor God with our first fruit and any other charitable donations. The second line is saving because we should be paying ourselves and investing in ourselves every pay period. We are wise people, and wise people save money. It's a crystal clear biblical principle.

I pray that all the negative Nancys and Debbie Downers are out of our ear gates and eye gates and that we have learned to stay away from these types of individuals who crush our dreams and visions. I pray that we are encouraging ourselves in the good news of the gospel and standing on the promises of God.

I pray that you have begun your budgets to begin tackling your debts and have opened up a savings account to at least start saving 10% of your monthly income. I also hope and pray that you all have begun to invest in yourself and your future.

* * *

***Prayer of Success and Purpose***

*Father God, we come to You today to say thank You. Thank You, God, that You give us brand-new mercies and grace every day. Thank You for Your unconditional love. Thank You, God, that Your yes and amen in heaven, is a yes and amen in the earth.*

*You said, God, that whatever we bind on earth shall be bound in heaven. So I bind the enemies' attack on our finances today, and I release discipline to have the ability to start saving and budgeting to secure our future.*

*I bind up double-mindedness, and I release a sound mind full of Your power, Your might, Your love, and the Holy Spirit helping us to exercise self-control and self-discipline in the area of finances and our daily walk with You, God.*

*I bind up procrastination and that lazy spirit trying to keep us in a place of lack and in a poverty mindset. I release a spirit of enthusiasm and a spirit of "I can do all things through Christ Jesus, who strengthens me."*
*Lord, release upon us the spirit of "I think I can, I know I can, and I will succeed."*

*We place our plans before You, Lord, for we know in Your word that with You as the head of our life, plans, goals, dreams, and vision, they will succeed according to what You have purposed for us.*

*So, God, we thank You that we can cast all of our burdens, insecurities, anxieties, and fears upon You, God, knowing that You have all power in Your Hands:*

- *Power to heal*
- *Power to set us free*
- *Power to deliver us from the enemies' snares*
- *Power to deliver us from ourselves, from speaking negativity and death to our very lives and existence*
- *Power to deliver us from people, places, and things that may be hindering us from the many blessings and overflow of blessings that You have for us*

*Lord, as I stand in the gap and intercede for Your people today, God, remove anything that is not like You from our lives. Help us to forgive others and show loving-kindness to all You bring in our paths. Give us a kind word, a loving heart, a listening ear, and a smile that will encourage Your people to keep moving forward.*

*Many people suffer from depression during this season. I bind up depression and send it back to the pits of hell from whence it came. I release Your peace, joy, happiness, and unity in its place, Lord God.*

*Help us to let go of all disappointments, failures, past hurts, and those things that are keeping us in bondage and pulling us away from the joy that only You can give, not the joys of this world, but the everlasting and eternal joy of Your Son Jesus that he left with us to comfort and heal our broken places.*

*Your joy is our strength when we become weak.*
*For, God, we do get weary, worn, and we do get tired.*
*But You said in Your Word, God, for us not to get weary in well doing*

*for in due season, we shall reap a harvest of much fruit if we faint not. Strengthen us, God, by Your power, Your might, and Your Holy Spirit. Many of us are missing our loved ones who have passed on before us. Lord God, comfort our hearts, relax our minds, and give us rest in Your loving arms as we release the tears of our burdened hearts. God, Your words say that You collect our tears to water our gardens later. Release the heaviness of our hearts and fill us up with joy. Help us to see that even in our low places, You are with us. You promised to never leave us nor forsake us.*

*Help us to realize that every day is a day of thanksgiving, a day to give to others our time, talents, and our treasure, realizing that the best gift to give, we already have in our possession—giving of our face-to-face time with one another.*

*Help us to move into this new decade with new determination:*

- *Determined to set a monthly budget*
- *Determined to make an aggressive plan to get out of debt and start saving and investing in our future*

*Father God, helps us to open up our hearts, eyes, ears, and our mouths and speak life and encouragement to ourselves and others around us.*

*Deliver us from gossip and noise, from wanting to be like the Joneses. Help us to be more mindful of our own lives and the things we need to do to be successful, healthy, wealthy, and wise. Help us to walk upright and stay on the path You have for our lives, the path we know to be narrow. Narrow is the way to God's heart and living a Kingdom-purposed life full of abundance, overflow, wealth, riches, love, kindness, unity, peace, and all the fruit of the Spirit.*

*Deliver us from Broad Street, living our lives any old kind of way, using our words to hurt others and tear them down, spreading discord among our brethren, and using intimidation tactics with one another.*

*Help us to recognize the Jezebel characteristics of a person: control, pride, arrogance, rejection, insecurity, and manipulation (reading Matthew 2:1–8, 16 [KJV] and Revelation 2:20 [KJV]).*

*God, as we close out this fiscal year, bring us into a place of quietness, a place where we can hear from You and follow the leading and guiding of Your Holy Spirit to guide and comfort our hearts, trusting You, God, and knowing You have our best interest at heart, knowing that You love us and forgive us of our sins as we confess to You, God, our sins of omission or commission.*

*Assist us in finding a place to reflect on the things that are of importance to us and our family. Help us to remember that we our free. Jesus paid the price at Calvary. All debts are paid in full in Jesus's name. Release the debts, whether they are financial or from persons. Release unto us, God, Your peace. In this decade of 2020s, the year of vision, the year of the open mouth, the year of our destiny being fulfilled, the year of "Yes, I can," the year of "Lord, I give You my yes," the year of "Let's go get it," the decade of moving forward together and together we grow. Renew us, restore us, and rebuild us on a solid foundation.*

*We seal these prayers in accordance with Jesus' Blood and Righteousness. Amen.*

# FINAL THOUGHTS FROM THE AUTHOR

> Refuse good advice and watch your plans fail; take good counsel and watch them succeed.
>
> — PROVERBS 15:22 MSG

This brings us to the close of "Take Ownership." I pray that you will go back and review the detailed information on how to manage your resources, protect your credit reports, and protect your identities from scammers, fraud, and identity theft. I also pray that you and your household will apply the ten steps to completing your financial portfolios. May you and your household focus on savings and investments to grow you exponentially and leave an inheritance for your children's children, in Jesus' authority.

May the legacy you leave behind speak to generations to come. May your future explode in prosperity and abundance as you apply the principles and precepts shared with you in my books:

- Volume 1 Book: *The Art of Budgeting*
- Volume 1 Journal: *The Journey to Financial Freedom Journal*
- Volume 2 Book: *Take Ownership*

We want to be ready for retirement and live a comfortable life after we retire. I look forward to hearing and receiving some of your testimonies as to how God has blessed your finances, multiplied your households, and increased your capacity and ability to create Kingdom wealth.

Once you and your household receive the blessing of God, be sure to share and care and show love, which is something we can truly afford to share more—love and forgiveness toward one another.

May God bless you and keep you in perfect peace. And remember to cast all our cares on God, for He cares for each and every one of us. Let's remember to lay our burdens at the feet of Jesus and leave them there. Be blessed…be encouraged…and know you are not alone. We all must become good stewards of our financial matters and our credit reports.

Be sure to check out our YouTube channel: Trifold Connections (https://youtube.com/@trifoldconnections3835). Like, subscribe, and hit the little bell to receive notifications when *Money Matters Mondays* airs on Monday evenings (7:30 p.m. CST). This is a free, education broadcast aired on all of our social media platforms.

> "There must be no poor people among you because God is going to bless you lavishly in this land that God, your God, is giving you as an inheritance, your very own land. But only if you listen obediently to the Voice of God, your God, diligently observing every commandment that I command you today. Oh yes-God, your God, will bless you just as he promised. You will lend to many nations but won't borrow from any; you'll rule over many nations but none will rule over you.
>
> — DEUTERONOMY 15:4–6 MSG

*Can God trust you with your wealth?*

# ACKNOWLEDGMENTS

I want to take this opportunity to acknowledge those individuals and places of business who have been so extremely supportive, kind, compensating, and encouraging to me while being creative to write my books. I thank God for divine connections!

It takes quietness and a welcoming environment to be creative and release what instructions I receive from the Holy Spirit to put on the pages of my manuscripts.

* * *

*I have to start by thanking my beautifully gifted and talented daughters, Patricia and LaTascha Savage.* The two of you have been my biggest supporters and have encouraged me to stay the course. I have found renewed strength and courage to continue to step out on faith and to follow my dreams and the vision God has given me. Thank you, Pat and Tascha. Momma loves you, and I thank you for always being there to listen, give suggestions, show unconditional love and affection, and pray for Momma through every possible situation. God pulled us through together and strengthened our relationship and family values. "We try harder."

*I am eternally grateful to my pastors, Drs. Bill and Veronica Winston* of Living Word Christian Center (Forest Park, IL) who have inspired me to "keep walking by faith," to believe in the impossible being made possible through Christ Jesus, to dream bigger, to put the Word of God on the things I am believing God for, and most of all for their leadership and prayers. Thank you for bar-none leadership, direction, and trailblazing (www.lwcc.org).

*To the foundational members of Tri Fold Connections,* I am forever grateful and thankful for the time, talent, and treasure that you share with Tri Fold Connections. I remember when I was asked about my team. I asked God, "God, where is my team?" In August 2021, the team of foundational members was formed, and God is increasing the number of foundational members He selected to be midwives and doctors to aid and assist in birthing this enormous vision to fruition. Thank you for the professional gifts you bring to the table: your understanding, your financial gifts, your diversity, and your unconditional love. I will forever love each and every one of you. May God continue to grow you exponentially. In Jesus's authority, amen.

*To Camille McMickle, aka CamilleSings,* the "voice" of Tri Fold Connections, I remember when the Holy Spirit led me to contact you to ask if you would become the "voice" of Tri Fold Connections. You were so excited, and without hesitation, you accepted the invitation. I love your music. It has soothed my mind, body, soul, and spirit many days and nights. I was truly going through some growing pains in 2019 when God had me birth the vision of Tri Fold Connections. My process of being developed into who God predestined me to become was grueling and very lonely at times, but your music spoke volumes to my heart, as if God Himself was soothing my Spirit through your voice. I know that each one of your songs is inspired by the Holy Ghost and backed by the Holy Bible. Your voice is likened to an angelic sound, and when you stroke the strings of your guitar, it makes heavenly music. I thank you for your love and encouragement, our long heart-to-heart talks, your time, talents, gifts, understanding, and your willingness and dedication to God and Tri Fold Connections. I truly thank you for your heartfelt prayers. I love you!(www.CamilleSings.com)

*I must give accolades to Mrs. Alison Cunningham of AC Creatives.* I thank you for your creativity and brilliant mind. I love that I can call you, express the vision, and you go consult the Holy Spirit for directions and instructions on how to create all the marketing advertisements and course materials and assist with administrative tasks for Tri Fold Connections. I love that every meeting we have begins and ends with prayer. You are a precious and rare diamond to me and Tri Fold Connections as a whole. When I wanted to give up, you pressed in prayer and encouraged me to stay strong, stay focused, and stay the course. We sometimes had times of separation, but you always put the calling and assignment on your life first. I am so thankful and grateful for your friendship, unconditional love, and support. Your professional work is exceptional and cutting-edge. I thank you for all you do behind the scenes for me and Tri Fold Connections. Sister Alison Cunningham, I love you. (Email: contact@mrsalisoncunningham.com; 1440 West Taylor Street, Suite 835, Chicago, Illinois, 60607; 773-362-5466.)

*To my publisher, Nicole Queen of Vision Publishing House,* you took the guesswork out of the equation. Writing a book takes diligence, dedication, and determination. With your level of expertise, you kept me focused on content building. You held my hand and literally walked me through becoming a brand-new author. You prayed for me when I needed to be uplifted the most. You became more than a publisher to me. You became my friend and an honorary foundational member of Tri Fold Connections. I thank you for your encouragement, leadership, and your prayers. (Contact: nicole@vision-publishinghouse.com; www.vision-publishinghouse.com)

*Now, to the team at Natchez Manor Bed & Breakfast* at 600 Franklin Street, Natchez, Mississippi, 39120. This is owned by Eric Berry, with Emily McNeill as the business manager, Annie Rose Jones as manager and lead chef, and Justin Brown as host. I honor you and commend you for your five-star hotel and hospitality. The atmosphere is so warm and welcoming. I cannot describe the peace I have when working long hours in the La Salle room. Mrs. Rose and Justin are always providing excellent service with a smile. I take this opportunity to thank you for accommodating all my needs and trusting me in your establishment. Most times I have the entire B&B to myself, and I love it. You are my family, and Natchez Manor is my home away from home. I will always be so indebted to you for your tender love and care that you have shown me. Mrs. Rose, I love you and call you a friend. I will be calling you soon to have my room ready for there are more books to come. Thank you to the owner and staff of Natchez Manor B&B. (Contact: info@natchezmanor.-com; 601-442-4441; www.natchezmanor.com)

*Last but surely not least, to the Mayor of Natchez, MI, Dan M. Gibson,* I will forever honor and appreciate you for your hospitality, encouragement, and admiration. When first meeting you through Dr. Myers, your first response when you heard I was a prophet was to ask me to pray for you and the city of Natchez. I remember standing in your office, holding hands in the posture of prayer, praying God's blessing over you and the beautiful city of Natchez. I have witnessed the economic growth and development you have brought to the city of Natchez through much prayer and supplication. May God show His favor upon you and all of your endeavors for God's people as you bring restoration and hope to the families, businesses, and the county seat of Adams County. Thank you, Mayor Dan M. Gibson. I will always have a special place in my heart for your love and kindness. You are appreciated!

# ABOUT THE AUTHOR

Henrietta England is an esteemed financial service consultant who has found much success at Trifold Connections LLC. She began her career in 1983 as a customer service representative and credit consultant for the Nelson Brothers Furniture Company. Soon thereafter, she garnered over 10 years of experience as a senior banker and mortgage loan officer at LaSalle Bank and Bank of America. Prior to her current role, she excelled as the Vice President and Branch Manager at Standard Bank and Trust. She recently concluded her lengthy tenure at Ford Motor Company and is now enjoying her retirement

Currently, she manages the day-to-day functions at Tri Fold Connections LLC. She produces weekly broadcasts within her "Money Matters Mondays" series, which are educational programs that can be viewed virtually on YouTube, LinkedIn, Twitter, Facebook, Twitch, and her website.

Henrietta truly enjoys educating others to help them move forward to financial freedom, abundance, and overflow. She utilizes Biblical principles and precepts in financial literacy, economic growth, and development to help individuals build kingdom wealth, God's way!

*Many of her accomplishments include:*

- Celebrated for Excellence In Financial Advising and Education (March 2023)
- Honoree, Distinguished Worldwide Humanitarian Award (2022)
- Recipient of Albert Nelson Marquis - Lifetime Achievement Award (2021); Published in Wall Street Journal December 8th, 2021, edition
- Featured Member, Marquis Millennium Magazine, Marquis - -- Who's Who (July 2022)
- Honoree, Number One, Community Reinvestment Area, for Working with Low to Moderate Income Buyers, LaSalle Bank (2008, 2007, 2006)
- Certificate, Top Mortgage Loan Originator, LaSalle Bank
- Honoree, Top Producer and Manager, Standard Bank and Trust
- Recipient, Top Banker Awards
- Third Place, State of Colorado in Finance and Credit

*Stay connected!*

youtube.com/@trifoldconnections3835
facebook.com/trifoldconnections
instagram.com//trifoldconnections

Life is short; *live it*
Love is rare; *grab it*
Anger is bad; *dump it*
Fear is awful; f*ace it*
Memories are sweet; c*herish them*

— Author Unknown

www.ingramcontent.com/pod-product-compliance
Lightning Source LLC
Chambersburg PA
CBHW041300210926
51847CB00009B/82
*9781955297516*